# THE PEOPLE OF
# Moray, Banff, and Nairn
## 1700 - 1799

By
David Dobson

Copyright © 2019
by David Dobson
All Rights Reserved

Printed for Clearfield Company by
Genealogical Publishing Company
Baltimore, Maryland
2019

ISBN 9780806358840

THE PEOPLE OF MORAY, BANFF, AND NAIRN, 1700-1799

INTRODUCTION

Moray lies between the Moray Firth and the Grampian mountains, and is comprised of a fertile coastal plain with river valleys, such as the Spey. The major families or clans in the district included Gordons, Grants, Innes, Dunbar, Rose, Leslie, Fordyce, Brodie, Geddes, and Ogilvie. The district of Moray now includes the former adjacent counties of Banff and Nairn.

The area known as the District of Moray is roughly the area covered by the old Celtic province of that name, dating from the Pictish period. In 1130 the Mormaer [Earl] of Moray and his followers rebelled against the rule of King David I of Scotland based in Edinburgh. King David suppressed the revolt with the assistance of Flemish knights who had settled in Scotland. These knights, men such as Freskin and Berewald, were granted the lands of the rebels. The knights mostly adopted the names of the lands as their surnames, thus founding several notable Scottish families such as Murray, Innes, and Duffus, while some used Fleming as their surname. A branch of the Dunbar family from south-east Scotland also settled there.

The medieval period in Moray witnessed the construction of castles and religious houses at Pluscarden, Kinloss, Bernie, Elgin, Duffus and Dallas. By the early modern period the main settlements and burghs in Moray were Forres, Nairn, Auldearn, Findhorn, Spynie, and especially Elgin. Moray's economy was based on agriculture, fishing, and trade. Vessels traded from the ports of Moray to Scandinavia, the Baltic, the Netherlands, England, and on occasion to the Americas. These trading links facilitated emigration. The roughly 1,200 Moray inhabitants identified here may be the antecedents of persons living in those countries today.

David Dobson

Dundee, Scotland, 2018

THE PEOPLE OF MORAY, BANFF, AND NAIRN, 1700-1799

ABBOT, Captain, of Lossiemouth, was admitted as a burgess of Elgin in 1786. [EBR]

ABERCROMBY, ARTHUR, was appointed to a Dutch East India Ship bound for China in 1758. [NRS.NRAS,0002]

ABERCROMBIE, BESSIE, widow of Dr James Hay former minister of Elgin, testament, 21 September 1790, Comm. Aberdeen. [NRS]

ABERCROMBY, GEORGE, son of Alexander Abercromby of Nether Skeith, Banffshire, a Jacobite in 1715. [JNE.1]

ABERCROMBY, GEORGE, a brother of Sir George Abercromby of Birkenbog, a doctor in Mexico around 1770, father of John, an officer in the Spanish Army, and Mary Louise. [NRS.NRAS.0002]

ABERCROMBY, Sir JAMES, of Birkenbog, born 1669, son of Sir Alexander Abercromby, a Jacobite in 1715. [JNE.1]

ABERCROMBY, JAMES, a farmer in Skeith, Banffshire, husband of Elspeth Ord, daughter of a merchant in Cullen, a Jacobite in 1745. [JNE/2.1]

ABERCROMBY, Colonel JAMES, in Fordyce, 1753. [NRS.E326.1.17]

ABERCROMBY, Sir ROBERT, in Fordyce, 1753. [NRS.E326.1.17]

ABERNETHY, GEORGE, master of the Peggie of Banff trading with Newcastle and Kirkcaldy in 1752. [NRS.E504.1.4]

ABERNETHY, JOHN, master of the Rothiemay of Banff trading between Newcastle, England, and Aberdeen in 1743, [NRS.E504.1.1]; trading between Rotterdam, Zealand, and Inverness in 1745, [NRS.E504.17.1]; trading with Newcastle, Rotterdam, and Lisbon, Portugal, in 1747-1748, [NRS.E504.1.2]; trading with Newcastle and Lisbon on 1749-1751. [NRS.E504.1.3]; master of the Happy Return of Banff trading with Bo'ness and Rotterdam in 1751-1752. [NRS.E504.1.4]; master of the Rothiemay of Banff trading with Bumblefjord, Norway, Sunderland, England, and Newcastle, England, in 1751-1752. [NRS.E504.1.4]

# THE PEOPLE OF MORAY, BANFF, AND NAIRN, 1700-1799

ABERNETHIE, JOHN, son of Captain John Abernethie in Bengal, India, admitted as a burgess of Banff in 1777. [BBF]

ADAM, ALEXANDER, a chapman in Unthank of Urquhart, was admitted as a burgess of Elgin in 1756. [EBR]

ADAM, ALEXANDER, formerly a merchant in Elgin, later in Aberdeen, testament, 14 September 1799, Comm. Aberdeen. [NRS]

ADAM, JOHN, a grave-maker in Elgin, died in 1763. [RE.2.345]

ADAM, WILLIAM, in Newmiln, was admitted as a burgess of Elgin in 1761. [EBR]

ADAM, WILLIAM, a chapman, was admitted as a burgess of Elgin in 1774. [EBR]

ADAMSON, JOHN, master of the sloop Jean of Banff, bound from Banff to Trontheim, Norway, in April 1807. [NRS.E504.5.1]

ALAN, BENJAMIN, servant to Lord Grange, was admitted as a burgess of Elgin in 1709. [EBR]

ALLAN, ALEXANDER, jr., a merchant in Garmouth, was admitted as a burgess of Elgin in 1751. [EBR]

ALLAN, ALEXANDER, son of Robert Allan a merchant, was admitted as a burgess of Elgin in 1775. [EBR]

ALLAN, DAVID, master of the David of Portsoy trading with Danzig in 1750. [NRS.E504.1.3]

ALLAN, JAMES, in Main, was admitted as a burgess of Elgin in 1774. [EBR]

ALLAN, JAMES, a merchant in Buckie, testament, 7 May 1788, Comm. Aberdeen. [NRS]

ALLAN, JOHN, from Forres, married Helena Blankert from Rotterdam, Zealand, in the Scots Kirk in Rotterdam on 17 May 1738. [Rotterdam Archives]

ALLAN, JOHN, a farmer in Mossie, Banff, a Jacobite in 1745. [JNE.2.2]

## THE PEOPLE OF MORAY, BANFF, AND NAIRN, 1700-1799

ALLAN, JOHN, master of the Magnet of Banff trading with Riga, Latvia, in 1806. [NRS.E504.5.1]

ALLAN, THOMAS, a church elder in Elgin in 1701 and 1709. [RE.2.325/328]

ALLANOCH, JOHN, a merchant in Clashmore, Banff, a Jacobite in 1745. [JNE.2.2]

ALLASTER, PETER, master of the Fancy of Banff trading between Aberdeen, Rotterdam, and Belfast in 1743 -1745. [NRS.E504.1.1]; master of the Well Met of Portsoy trading with Danzig in 1747. [NRS.E504.1.2]

ALVES, ALEXANDER, son of Alexander Alves a farmer, was admitted as a burgess of Elgin on 21 September 1765. [EBR]

ALVES, JAMES, a church elder in Elgin in 1709. [RE.2.328]

ALVES, JOHN, servant to baillie Leslie, was admitted as a burgess of Elgin in 1775. [EBR]

ANDERSON, ALEXANDER, a servant in Upper Dallachy, Banffshire, a Jacobite in 1745. [JNE.2.2]

ANDERSON, ALEXANDER, a servant in Knockiemill, Banff, a Jacobite in 1745. [JNE.2.2]

ANDERSON, ALEXANDER, a shoemaker, was admitted as a burgess of Elgin in 1774. [EBR]

ANDERSON, ALEXANDER, born 25 February 1782, son of Reverend Joseph Anderson and his wife Jean Craig in Birnie, died aboard the Hercules in the West Indies in September 1803. [F.6.380]

ANDERSON, ARCHIBALD, born 10 June 1785, son of Reverend Joseph Anderson and his wife Jean Craig in Birnie, a surgeon of the Honourable East India Company, died in 1817. [F.6.380]

## THE PEOPLE OF MORAY, BANFF, AND NAIRN, 1700-1799

ANDERSON, GEORGE, a surgeon in Honourable East India Company Service in 1787, grandson of George Anderson a merchant in Forres, a sasine. [NRS.RS.Caithness.85]

ANDERSON, HUGH, born 1666, son of Reverend Hugh Anderson in Cromarty, graduated MA from Edinburgh University in 1683, minister at Rosemarkie in 1694, then at Drainie from 1698 until 1740, he died on 26 October 1749. Husband of Margaret Munro. [F.6.383]

ANDERSON, JAMES, a brasier, was admitted as a burgess of Elgin in 1723. [EBR]

ANDERSON, JAMES, of Linkwood, Provost of Elgin, from 1729 to 1731. [RE.2.477]

ANDERSON, JAMES, from Bellie, Moray, a Jacobite in 1745, transported to the colonies in 1747. [JNE.2.2]

ANDERSON, JAMES, a merchant in Upper Dalachie, Banff, an Ensign in the Jacobite army in 1745. [JNE.2.2]

ANDERSON, JAMES, a cooper in Findhorn, husband of Janet McQueen, sasine, 1780. [NRS.RS29.8.457]

ANDERSON, JAMES, a mason in Forres, 1785. [NRS.E746.45]

ANDERSON, JAMES, born 1789 in Cullen, Banffshire, a member of the firm Anderson, Wallace, and Company, died 24 April 1843, husband of Margaret, born 1805 in Cullen, died 16 March 1843. [Scotch Burial Ground gravestone, Calcutta, India.]

ANDERSON, JAMES, jr., a merchant in Forres, 1797. [NRS.CS228.A6.55]

ANDERSON, JAMES, a skipper in Macduff, testament, 1804, Comm. Aberdeen. [NRS]

ANDERSON, JEAN, in Buckie, widow of Robert Bremner, testament, 14 November 1775, Comm. Aberdeen. [NRS]

THE PEOPLE OF MORAY, BANFF, AND NAIRN, 1700-1799

ANDERSON, JOHN, from Boharm, Banffshire, a surgeon in St Michael's parish Barbados, probate 2 December 1714, Barbados. [RB6.41.9]

ANDERSON, JOHN, an armourer, was admitted as a burgess of Elgin in 1715. [EBR]

ANDERSON, JOHN, a gentleman in Craighead, Marnoch, Banffshire, an Ensign of the Jacobite army in 1745. [JNE.2.2]

ANDERSON, JOHN, a wright in Fochabers, a sasine, 1769. [NRS.RS29.8.195]

ANDERSON, Dr JOHN, in St Kitts, a sasine, 23 July 1792. [NRS.RS.Banff.292]

ANDERSON, JOSEPH, was educated at Marischal College, Aberdeen, from 1754 until 1758, schoolmaster of Alves from 1756 to 1765, minister of Birnie from 1766 until his death on 2 June 1808. Husband of Jean Craig, parents of Christian, Margaret, Jean, Alexander, Marjory, Archibald, Janet, and Anne. [F.6.380]

ANDERSON, MARGARET, in Elgin, 29 September 1702. [RE.2.326]

ANDERSON, ROBERT, a merchant in Elgin, son of baillie Robert Anderson, was admitted as a burgess of Elgin in 1705. [EBR]

ANDERSON, WILLIAM, of Linkwood, Provost of Elgin, from 1740 to 1743. [RE.2.477]

ANDERSON, WILLIAM, a merchant in Cullen, testament, 16 April 1781, Comm. Aberdeen. [NRS]

ANDERSON, WILLIAM, a square-wright, was admitted as a burgess of Elgin in 1769. [EBR]

ANDERSON, WILLIAM, was admitted as a burgess of Elgin in 1782. [EBR]

ANDERSON, WILLIAM, son of James Anderson of Mathiemilne, a sasine, 1780. [NRS.RS29.8.54]

## THE PEOPLE OF MORAY, BANFF, AND NAIRN, 1700-1799

ANDERSON, ......., emigrated from Moray to Prince Edward Island aboard the John and Elizabeth in 1775, shipwrecked in the Flat River, PEI. [TIM.18.30]

ANGUS, WALTER, and his wife Janet Forbes, in Fochabers, formerly at the Mill of Fochabers, a sasine, 1709. [NRS.RS29.5.88]

APPIE, JOHN, a weaver, was admitted as a burgess of Elgin in 1760. [EBR]

ARNOT, WILLIAM, son of William Arnot, a farmer in Elgin, was admitted as a burgess of Elgin in 1762. [EBR]

BAGRA, JEAN, widow of John Brodie a mason in Portsoy, testament, 17 March 1791, Comm. Aberdeen. [NRS]

BAILLIE, ...., was admitted as a burgess of Elgin on 2 September 1731. [EBR]

BAIN, HUGH, a tailor, was admitted as a burgess of Elgin in 1758. [EBR]

BAIN, JOHN, the younger, from Glen Conglass, Banffshire, a Jacobite in 1745. [JNE.2.3]

BAIN-STEWART, ARCHIBALD, from Delavorar, Banffshire, a Jacobite in 1745. [JNE.2.3]

BAIRD, GEORGE, in Linkwood, a disposition in favour of Robert Allan a merchant in Elgin, 30 November 1742. [NRS.CS228D.1.5.2]

BAIRD, WILLIAM, a merchant in Elgin, versus Thomas Stephen jr. a merchant in Elgin, also John Jamieson, a merchant in Elgin, a poinding, 1764. [NRS.CS228.B4.60]

BANNERMAN, JAMES, in Forgland, 1748. [NRS.E326.1.17]

BARCLAY, JOHN, a shoemaker from Fochaber, Moray, a Jacobite in 1745. [JNE.2.4]

BARON, JOHN, a shoemaker, was admitted as a burgess of Elgin in 1760. [EBR]

BARRON, ROBERT, in Gamry, 1748. [NRS.E326.1.17]

THE PEOPLE OF MORAY, BANFF, AND NAIRN, 1700-1799

BARTLE, JAMES, a shoemaker in Fochabers, a sasine 1709. [NRS.RS20.5.25]

BARTLET, JAMES, in Gardenstoun, testament, 12 August 1800, Comm. Aberdeen. [NRS]

BATCHIN, JAMES, in Elgin, versus John Jamieson a merchant in Elgin, a suspension, 1790. [NRS.CS228.B7.63]

BAXTER, MARJORY, spouse of John Davidson, to be rebuked for calling Isabel Thomson a witch, in Elgin in 1706. [RE.2.327]

BELL, BENJAMIN, a Chelsea pensioner, a tack of Robertsfield, Forres, 1 October 1755. [NRS.GD248.533.2.60]

BENNAGAGH, JOHN, from Banffshire, a Jacobite imprisoned in Carlisle in 1746. [ANE.2.4]

BENNET, ROBERT, a merchant in Fochabers, a Jacobite in 1745. [JNE.2.4]

BEZACK, JOHN, a mason in Forres, later in Leith, 1797. [NRS.CS228.A6.55]

BEZACH, WILLIAM, a tenant in Linguishton, Forres, 1779. [NRS.GD248.533.5.78]

BIB, ALEXANDER, a merchant in Forres, husband of Florence Keir, a sasine, 1727. [NRS.RS29.6.314]

BICKLEY, JAMES, an apprentice miller at the mill of Turriff, Banff, a Jacobite in 1745. [JNE.2.4]

BLACK, ALEXANDER, in Bishopmill, husband of Elspeth Allan, a sasine, 1711. [NRS.RS29.5.235]

BLACK, CHARLES, a writer in Forres, 1800. [NRS.CS228.B11.46]

BLACK, GEORGE, son of Michael Black, was admitted as a burgess of Elgin in 1714. [EBR]

## THE PEOPLE OF MORAY, BANFF, AND NAIRN, 1700-1799

BLAIR, DAVID, master of the Jean of Banff trading with Alloa and with Veere, Zealand, in 1749-1750. [NRS.E504.1.3]

BLANE, ROBERT, a Lieutenant Colonel in Honourable East India Company Service, a sasine, 4 June 1792. [NRS.RS.Elgin/Forres.328]

BLENSHELL, WILLIAM, a shoemaker, was admitted as a burgess of Elgin in 1766. [EBR]

BOWER, JAMES, a butcher in Elgin, versus Thomas Imlach, a packman in Forres, 1758. [NRS.CS228.B4.28]

BOWAR, WILLIAM, a blacksmith, was admitted as a burgess of Elgin in 1769. [EBR]

BOWIE, JAMES, a brewer and maltster in Cullen, a Jacobite in 1745. [JNE.2.4]

BOWIE, JAMES, from Glenlivet, a Jacobite in 1745. [JNE.2.4]

BOWIE, ROBERT, from Parkmore, Banffshire, a Jacobite in 1745. [JNE.2.4]

BOWIE, ROBERT, a merchant in Bordeaux, France, a sasine, 23 April 1785. [NRS.RS.29.123]

BOWMAN, JAMES, from Portsoy, Banffshire, a Jacobite in 1745. [JNE.2.5]

BOYD, THOMAS, a merchant in Forres, a sasine, 7 December 1716. [NRS.RS28.110.151]

BOYN, ALEXANDER, a weaver, was admitted as a burgess of Elgin in 1760. [EBR]

BRACO, ....., was admitted as a burgess of Elgin in 1719. [EBR]

BRACO, ......., jr., was admitted as a burgess of Elgin on 11 September 1731. [EBR]

BRADLEY, JOHN, sometime in Fordyce, testament, 12 October 1750, Comm. Aberdeen. [NRS]

BRAND, JAMES, in Cullen, 1748. [NRS.E326.1.17]

BRAND, WALTER, a merchant and late bailie of Cullen, father of Ann Brand, testament, 24 June 1747, Comm. Aberdeen. [NRS]

BRANDER, ALEXANDER, was admitted as a burgess of Elgin in 1768. [EBR]

BRANDER, ALEXANDER, a merchant, provost of Elgin from 1792 to 1795, and from 1798 to 1799. [RE.2.477]

BRANDER, ANDREW, son of Andrew Brander a merchant, was admitted as a burgess of Elgin in 1760. [EBR]

BRANDER, JAMES, from Banff, a Jacobite who died aboard the Thane of Fife a prisoner bound for London in September 1746. [JNE.2.5]

BRANDER, JAMES, son of James Brander in Sheriffmiln, merchant, was admitted as a burgess of Elgin in 1757. [EBR]

BRANDER, JAMES, a merchant in Lisbon, Portugal, son of James Brander a merchant in Elgin, 1758. [NRS.RS29.VII.409]

BRANDER, JAMES, son of baillie Alexander Brander, was admitted as a burgess of Elgin in 1775. [EBR]

BRANDER, JOHN, son of John Brander, merchant, was admitted as a burgess of Elgin in 1755. [EBR]

BRANDER, JOHN, son of Andrew Brander, merchant, was admitted as a burgess of Elgin in 1758. [EBR]

BRANDER, JOHN, second son of Alexander Brander sr., merchant, was admitted as a burgess of Elgin in 1768. [EBR]

BRANDER, JOHN, in London, was admitted as a burgess of Elgin in 1785. [EBR]

BRANDER, WILLIAM, son of Alexander Brander, merchant in Elgin, was admitted as a burgess of Elgin in 1758. [EBR]

## THE PEOPLE OF MORAY, BANFF, AND NAIRN, 1700-1799

BREMNER, ALEXANDER, in Fordyce, 1753. [NRS.E326.1.17]

BREMNER, ALEXANDER, born 1793, son of James Bremner, a farmer, and his wife Isobel Ord, died in Demerara on 14 February 1820. [Speymouth Dipple gravestone]

BREMNER, GEORGE, a wright in Carnousie, a Jacobite in 1745. [JNE.2.5]

BREMNER, GEORGE, a shoemaker in Fochabers, a Jacobite in 1745. [JNE.2.5]

BREMNER, HELEN, relict of John Frigg a merchant in Findhorn, a sasine, 1750. [NRS.RS29.7.434]

BREMNER, JAMES, a baker, was admitted as a burgess of Elgin in 1776. [EBR]

BREMNER, JOHN, born 1792, son of Joseph Bremner, a feuar in Fochabers, and his wife Mary Allan, a mariner later a merchant in Nassau, New Providence, the Bahamas, died there on 30 August 1818. [Bellie gravestone]

BREMNER, JOSEPH, born 1799, son of Joseph Bremner, a feuar in Fochabers, and his wife Christina Ross, a merchant in Samarang, Java, died 13 May 1831 in Java. [Bellie gravestone]

BROCKIE, JAMES, a merchant in Fochabers, a sasine, 1747. [NRS.RS29.7.221]

BRODIE, ALEXANDER, of Windyhills, Provost of Elgin, from 1749 to 1752, 1755 to 1758, 1761 to 1764, 1767 to 1770, 1774 to 1775, 1778 to 1779. [RE.2.477]

BRODIE, ALEXANDER, born 1738, son of Alexander Brodie of Windyhills and his wife Ann Dawson, a merchant in Windyhills, St Mary's parish, Antigua, married Ann Kidder [1730-1801] in 1766, died in Antigua in 1800. [Caribbeana.i.98]

BRODIE, ALEXANDER, in Madras, India, was admitted as a burgess of Banff in 1785. [BBR]

THE PEOPLE OF MORAY, BANFF, AND NAIRN, 1700-1799

BRODIE, DAVID, a physician in Elgin, a sasine, 1725. [NRS.RS29.6.161]

BRODIE, EMILIA, widow of Captain John McLeod of McLeod, heir to her brother Alexander Brodie of Brodie who died in September 1759, 3 September 1773, lands in Elgin, Forres and Nairnshire. [NRS.S/H]

BRODIE, FRANCIS, of Inverlochty, the elder, a sasine, 1725. [NRS.RS29.6.165]

BRODIE, JAMES, of Brodie, MP for Nairnshire, a letter, 1797. [NRS.GD51.1.884]

BRODIE, JOHN, master of the Peace of Elgin trading with Veere, Zealand in 1750. [NRS.E504.1.3]

BRODIE, JOSEPH, of Miltown, a church elder in Elgin in 1746. [RE.2.385]

BRODIE, LOUISA, from Moray, wife of H. Cotton a surveyor in Van Diemen's Land from 1843 to 1850. [NRS.NRAS.0021]

BRODIE, WILLIAM, in Cotton of Glenbucket, eldest son of Alastair Brodie and his wife Jean Morris, husband of Jean Brebner, a Jacobite in 1745, died at Dalfrankie, Glenbucket, in 1776. [JNE.2.5]

BRODIE, WILLIAM, the British Consul in Malaga, Spain, was admitted as a burgess of Banff in 1799. [BBR]

BROWN, ALEXANDER, a vagabond in Banff Tolbooth, was released to enrol in Lieutenant General Collier's Regiment of the Scots Brigade in the service of Holland, on 4 May 1724. [RB.401]

BROWN, ANDREW, son of William Brown and his wife Marion Anderson in the Mill of Rubray, Forglen, Banffshire, a traveller in Germany in 1599. [MSC.II.48]

BROWN, JAMES, in Fordyce, 1753. [NRS.E326.1.17]

BROWN, Sir GEORGE, of Colston, was admitted as a burgess of Elgin in 1694. [EBR]

## THE PEOPLE OF MORAY, BANFF, AND NAIRN, 1700-1799

BROWN, GEORGE, factor to the Earl of Findlator, was admitted as a burgess of Elgin in 1780. [EBR]

BROWN, GEORGE, of Linkwood, Provost of Elgin, from 1782 to 1785, 1788 to 1791, 1795 to 1798, and 1799 to 1801. [RE.2.477]

BROWN, GORDON, MD, born 2 July 1784, son of Reverend Alexander Brodie and his wife Isabella Ord in Spynie, was educated at Marischal College, Aberdeen, from 1799 to 1802, a physician in Demerara, died there on 16 July 1813. [F.6.407][MCA]

BROWN, JAMES, a merchant in Portsoy, testament, 24 March 1792, Comm. Aberdeen. [NRS]

BROWN, JAMES, a skipper in Banff, testament, 1810, Comm. Aberdeen. [NRS]

BROWN, JAMES, born 1809, son of John Brown, a feuar in Fochabers, and his wife Helen Gray, died in New York in 1834. [Bellie gravestone]

BROWUN, JOHN, in Carnousie, Banffshire, a Jacobite in 1745. [JNE2.5]

BROUN, JOSEPH, born 1731, a tailor in Banff, a Jacobite in 1745, captured and transported bound for the Leeward Islands but released by a French privateer and landed on Martinique in 1747. [JNE.2.5]

BROWN, LOUISA, born 22 June 1795 in Spynie, daughter of Reverend Alexander Brown and his wife Isabel Ord, wife of William Willox, died in Sierra Leone on 21 March 1826. [F.6.407]

BROWN, WILLIAM, a servant at Carnousie Waulkmill near Banff, a Jacobite in 1745. [JNE.2.5]

BROWN, Captain, was admitted as a burgess of Elgin in 1785. [EBR]

BRUCE, ALEXANDER, a merchant in Banff, testament, 13 December 1781, Comm. Aberdeen. [NRS]

BRUCE, ALEXANDER, a merchant in Gardenstoun, testament, 13 November 1794, Comm. Aberdeen. [NRS]

BRUCE, JAMES, master of the Anne of Banff trading with Kirkcaldy, Fife, in 1747. [NRS.E504.1.2]; master of the Sarah of Gamry trading with Kirkcaldy, Alloa, and Bo'ness, in 1749-1750. [NRS.E504.1.3/4]; master of the Sarah of Banff trading with Bo'ness in 1749. [NRS.E504.1.3]

BRUCE JANET, relict of William Troup of Over Crookmuir, a sasine, 1705. [NRS.RS29.4.234]

BRUCE, SIMON, servant to Provost Robertson, was admitted as a burgess of Elgin in 1755. [EBR]

BRYANT, WILLIAM, in Kingston, Jamaica, was admitted as a burgess of Banff in 1774. [BBR]

BUCHANAN, HUGH, in Elgin, a letter, 20 August 1782. [NRS.CH12.24.411]

BUCHANAN, JOHN, from Banff, married Elizabeth McNeil, daughter of Neil McNeil, in the Scots Kirk in Rotterdam, Zealand, on 18 August 1763. [Rotterdam Archives]

BURD, JOHN, born in Portsoy on 24 September 1795, son of Charles Burd and his wife Mary Johnston, settled in Copenhagen, Denmark, in 1818, a shipmaster trading to the East Indies, married [1] Mette Marie Grefson on 7 October 1826, [2] Katie Caroline Winning, was appointed as Danish Consul in Hong Kong in 1845, died on 7 February 1855. [Danish East India Company, papers, Danish National Archives]

BURGESS, JAMES, a gunsmith in Elgin, a sasine, 1709. [NRS.RS29.5.7]

BURGESS, JAMES, son of William Burgess in Rothes who died in November 1831, settled in Demerara and Essequibo. [NRS.S/H.1867]

BURLEIGH, Mr, was admitted as a burgess of Elgin in 1786. [EBR]

BURNET, JAMES, in Batavia, Dutch East Indies, was admitted as a burgess of Banff in 1771. [BBR]

CALDER, ARCHIBALD, Commissary of Stores in Antigua, was admitted as a burgess of Banff in 1768. [BBR]

CALDER, JOHN, a tack of Deshar, Duthel, 31 March 1779. [NRS.GD248.533.2/83]

CAMERON, ALEXANDER, in Nairn, a Jacobite in 1745, was captured and transported to Barbados in 1747. [JNE.2.6]

CAMERON, JOHN, from Croftbain, Banffshire, a Jacobite in 1745. [JNE.2.6]

CAMPBELL, ANGUS, a carrier in Banff, a Jacobite in 1745. [JNE.2.6]

CAMPBELL, Sir ARCHIBALD, of Clunas, husband of Anna McPherson, a sasine, 1710. [NRS.RS29.5.125]

CAMPBELL, ARCHIBALD, minister in Grange, 1757. [NRS.E326.1.17]

CAMPBELL, DUNCAN, Collector of Supply for Nairnshire, letters, 1780s. [NRS.GD23.6.274]

CAMPBELL, GEORGE, minister in Bontripheny, 1757. [NRS.E326.1.17]

CAMPBELL, JAMES, in Dowan Vale, Jamaica, was admitted as a burgess of Banff in 1783. [BBR]

CAMPBELL, Colonel JOHN, was admitted as a burgess of Elgin in 1722. [EBR]

CAMPBELL, WILLIAM, master of the Jean of Banff arrived in Leith from Banff in July 1749. [NRS.CS96/1788]

CARMICHAEL, JANET, spouse of James Dunbar of Dunphail, a sasine, 1709. [NRS.RS29.5.93]

CARSTAIRS, ALEXANDER, in Rotterdam, Zealand, was admitted as a burgess of Elgin in 1686. [EBR]

CATTANACH, ANDREW, from Banff, a Jacobite captured at Culloden in 1746. [JNE.2.6]

CATTO, ALEXANDER, master of the James of Banff trading between Aberdeen and Trontheim, Norway, in 1743. [NRS.E504.1.1]

CHALMERS, FRANCIS, Episcopal minister in Elgin, a sasine 1747. [NRS.RS29.7.422]

CHALMER, JAMES, second son of George Chalmer the town clerk, was admitted as a burgess of Elgin in 1708. [EBR]

CHALMERS, JAMES, son of James Chalmers of Balnellan, Boharm, a planter in St Thomas in the Vale, Surrey County, Jamaica, 1766. [NRS.Consistorial Processes and Decreets]

CHAPE, JAMES, born 1726, a smith at St Marnoch, Banffshire, a Jacobite captured and transported to Port North Potomac, Maryland in 1747. [JNE.2.6]

CHAPMAN, JAMES, a gardener in Dun, Banffshire, a Jacobite captured and transported to Port Oxford, Maryland in 1747. [JNE.2.7]

CHARLES, JAMES, a merchant baillie of Elgin, a Jacobite in 1715, [RE.2.379], husband of Janet Innes, a sasine, 1726. [NRS.RS29.6.188]

CHALMERS, JOHN, a chapman, was admitted as a burgess of Elgin in 1766. [EBR]

CHALMERS, WILLIAM, a tailor, was admitted as a burgess of Elgin in 1774. [EBR]

CHAPMAN, JAMES, clerk, was admitted as a burgess of Elgin in 1785. [EBR]

CHRYSTIE, ALEXANDER, a gardener, was admitted as a burgess of Elgin in 1767. [EBR]

CHRYSTIE, WILLIAM, was admitted as a burgess of Elgin in 1782. [EBR]

CHRYSTIE, ALEXANDER, a servant, was admitted as a burgess of Elgin in 1771. [EBR]

CHRISTY, PATRICK, a farmer from Corsairtly, Banfshire, a Jacobite in 1745. [JNE.2.7]

CLAPPERTON, THOMAS, a weaver from Fochabers, Banffshire, a Jacobite captured and transported to Port Oxford, Maryland, in 1747. [JNE.2.7]

CLAPPERTON, WILLIAM, born 1734, son of Thomas Clapperton, a ploughboy, a Jacobite who was captured and transported to the West Indies, liberated by the French and landed on Martinique in 1747. [JNE.2.7]

CLARK, ALEXANDER, born 1670s, a skipper in Portsoy trading with Holland, a Jacobite in 1715, died 8 October 1732, testament, 8 April 1742, Comm. Aberdeen, [NRS][JNE.7]

CLARK, ALEXANDER, a dyster from Fochabers, a Jacobite in 1745. [JNE.2.7]

CLARK, ALEXANDER, a smith, was admitted as a burgess of Elgin in 1774. [EBR]

CLARK, BESSIE, spouse of John Shand in Garmouth, a sasine, 24 January 1717. [NRS.RS28.110.246]

CLARK, DAVID, a butler at Cullen House, was admitted as a burgess of Elgin in 1789. [EBR]

CLARK, ISABELL, daughter of Alexander Clark in the College of Elgin, and spouse of Robert Morison, a sasine, 31 May 1716. [NRS.RS28.109.103]

CLARK, ISOBELL, sometime in Banff, thereafter in Bredach, testament, 9 March 1758, Comm. Aberdeen. [NRS]

CLARK, JEAN, daughter of Alexander Clark in the College of Elgin, a sasine, 31 May 1716. [NRS.RS28.109.103]

CLARK, JOHN, a skipper from Portsoy, an assessor of the Scots Court in Veere, Zealand, in 1737, [NRS.RH11.2]; master of the <u>Fast Friend of</u>

THE PEOPLE OF MORAY, BANFF, AND NAIRN, 1700-1799

Portsoy trading between Inverness and Veere, Zealand, in 1742, trading between Aberdeen and Bergen, Norway, in 1743; and of the Providence of Portsoy trading between Aberdeen and Bergen, Norway, in 1744. [NRS.E504.1.1; E504.17.1]

CLARK, JOHN, a chapman, was admitted as a burgess of Elgin in 1752. [EBR]

CLARK, MARGARET, daughter of Alexander Clark in the College of Elgin, and spouse of Benjamin McKillandrea, a sasine, 31 May 1716. [NRS.RS28.109.103]

CLAVERING, ELIZABETH, born 1725, a seamstress in Banff, a Jacobite who was captured and transported to the Leeward Islands but was liberated by the French and landed on Martinique in 1747. [JNE.2.7]

CLAYTON, Captain JOSEPH, born 1781, died 18 May 1818 in Miramachi, Canada. [Banff gravestone]

CLERK, ALEXANDER, in the College of Elgin, father of Jean, Isabel, and Margaret, a sasine, Elgin and Forres, 1716. [NRS.RS3.109.103]

COBAN, ALEXANDER, a chapman in Monaughty, was admitted as a burgess of Elgin in 1779. [EBR]

COCK, JAMES, town clerk of Banff, testament, 10 July 1735, Comm. Aberdeen. [NRS]

COCKBURN, ALEXANDER, merchant in Banff, testament, 15 January 1754, Comm. Aberdeen. [NRS]

COLLIE, ALEXANDER, a writer in Elgin, 22 May 1790. [NRS.CS214.90]

COLLIE, JOHN, a merchant and Dean of Guild in Forres, spouse of Elspeth, a sasine 1712. [NRS.RS29.5.182]

COLLIE, WILLIAM, was educated at King's College, Aberdeen, graduated MA in 1718, schoolmaster in Drainie, from 1718 to 1734, a sasine, 1730. [NRS.RS29.6.286]; minister of Drainie from 1741 until his death on 29 April 1768. Husband of Margaret Mackenzie, parents of Margaret. [F.6.383]

COLLIE, WILLIAM, a farmer, was admitted as a burgess of Elgin in 1750. [EBR]

COOK, ALEXANDER, son of James Cook a shoemaker, was admitted as a burgess of Elgin in 1765. [EBR]

COOK, GEORGE, master of the Jean of Banff trading with Norway in 1749. [NRS.E504.1.3]

COOK, GEORGE, chapman in Coxton of Longbride, was admitted as a burgess of Elgin in 1752. [EBR]

COOK, JOHN, was admitted as a burgess of Elgin in 1782. [EBR]

COOK, THOMAS, a shoemaker in Cullen, testament, 26 March 1751, Comm. Aberdeen. [NRS]

COOK, WILLIAM, was admitted as a burgess of Elgin in 1782. [EBR]

CORDINER, CHARLES, Episcopal minister in Banff, testament,26 January 1795, Comm. Aberdeen. [NRS]

CORMIE, DAVID, was admitted as a burgess of Elgin in 1783. [EBR]

CORMIE, GEORGE, farmer at the East Port, was admitted as a burgess of Elgin on 21 September 1763. [EBR]

CORSE, JOHN, a saddler, was admitted as a burgess of Elgin in 1753. [EBR]

COULL, PATRICK, a merchant in Cullen, testament, 23 November 1784, Comm. Aberdeen. [NRS]

COUPLAND, JOHN, in Park, was appointed the Constable of Ordiewhill on 7 April 1741. [RB.409]

COW, GEORGE, post in Banff, testament, 22 July 1740, Comm. Aberdeen. [NRS]

COW, JOHN, a resident of Banff, was appointed post-master of Banffshire on 16 May 1720. [RB.398]

COWIE, ALEXANDER, a weaver in Fochabers, Moray, a Jacobite who was killed at the Battle of Culloden in 1746. [JNE.2.8]

COWIE, JAMES, a smith in Fochabers, 1709. [NRS.RS29.5.51]

CRAICK, ALEXANDER, master of the Success of Banff, trading with Newcastle, England, in 1753. [NRS.E504.1.4]

CRAIG, GEORGE, second son of Archibald Craig a merchant, was admitted as a burgess of Elgin in 1768. [EBR]

CRAIG, JAMES, was admitted as a burgess of Elgin in 1709. [EBR]

CRAMOND, JAMES, a church elder in Elgin in 1709. [RE.2.328]

CRAMOND, JAMES, a merchant bailie of Elgin, a disposition in favour of Janet Cramond, his eldest daughter, spouse of James Milne a merchant in Elgin on 17 February 1737. [NRS.CS228D.1.5.2]

CRAMOND, MARJORY, only child of the late James Cramond a merchant bailie of Elgin, a disposition in favour of her husband Robert Allan a merchant in Elgin, 17 December 1747. [NRS.CS228D.1.5.2]

CRAWFORD, CHARLES, born 1806, second son of Charles Crawford in Portsoy, a surgeon in the military hospital, Proto Medico of the Province of Chriquanas, died in Santa Cruz, Bolivia, in 1835. [AJ.4574]

CRAUFORD, PATRICK, in Rotterdam, Zealand, was admitted as a burgess of Banff in 1776. [BBR]

CRAWFORD, Lieutenant, of the Elgin Fencibles, married Miss English of Littlebridge, County Waterford, Ireland, on 4 October 1798. [SM.XL.729]

CROMBIE, JAMES, master of Elgin Grammar School in 1706, moved to Banff in 1709. [RE.2.410]

CROMBIE, WILLIAM, from Moray, a member of the Scots Charitable Society of Boston, Massachusetts, in 1745. [NEHGS; SCSms]

CRUDEN, JAMES, master of the James of Banff trading between Norway and Aberdeen in 1743; master of the James and Peggie of Banff trading between Aberdeen and Kirkcaldy, Fife, in 1744. [NRS.E504.1.1]; master of the Vernon of Banff trading with Newcastle, England, in 1748, and with Lisbon, Portugal, and Rotterdam, Zealand, in 1749. [NRS.E504.1.2/3]; trading between Inverness and Gothenburg, Sweden, in 1748. [NRS.E504.17.1]

CRUDEN, JAMES, master of the Music School, was admitted as a burgess of Elgin in 1758. [EBR]

CRUDEN, JOHN, was admitted as a burgess of Elgin in 1782. [EBR]

CRUICKSHANKS, ALEXANDER, from Banffshire, a member of the Scots Charitable Society of Boston, Massachusetts, in 1769. [NEHGS; SCS.ms]

CRUICKSHANKS, Captain CHARLES, in Haverford, Pennsylvania, later in Elgin, Moray, testament, 13 August 1785, Comm. Moray. [NRS]

CRUICKSHANK, JAMES, a merchant in Banff, testament, 26 September 1743. [NRS]

CRUICKSHANK, JOHN, a merchant in Banff, testament, 5 April 1750, Comm. Aberdeen. [NRS]

CRUICKSHANK, WILLIAM, a tack of Upper Gellovy, Duthil, in 1779. [NRS.GD248.533.3/63]

CRUICKSHANKS, WILLIAM, born 1775 in Moray, a shoemaker who settled in South Carolina, naturalised there on 15 August 1805. [NARA.M1163]

CUMMING, ALEXANDER, in the parish of Edinkillie, a contract, 7 March 1723. [NRS.GD36.33]

CUMMING, ALEXANDER, of Presley, and spouse Barbara, a sasine, 1726. [NRS.RS29.4.147]

CUMMING, ALEXANDER, son of Alexander Cumming a farmer in Pluscardine, was admitted as a burgess of Elgin in 1758. [EBR]

CUMMING, DAVID, of Presley, a sasine, 6 March 1716. [NRS.RS28.108.435]

CUMMING, GEORGE, was admitted as a burgess of Elgin in 1709. [EBR]

CUMMING, GEORGE, a merchant in Forres, accounts, 1797-1799. [NRS.GD248.240.5]

CUMMING, JAMES, servant to John Laing a merchant, was admitted as a burgess of Elgin in 1748. [EBR]

CUMMING, JAMES, a tack of Croft Chapel, Duthel, 1786. [NRS.GD248.533.3/33]

CUMMING, JANE, from Alvie, Moray, a Jacobite captured and transported to Port Oxford, Maryland, in 1747. [JNE.2.9]

CUMMING, JOHN, farmer in Solach of Dollas, was admitted as a burgess of Elgin in 1775. [EBR]

CUMMING, JOHN, of Pitlurg, heir to his grandfather Dr James Gordon of Pitlurg, who died in September 1754, to lands in Banffshire, 15 February 1774. [NRS.S/H]

CUMMING, LAUCHLAN, in Tomintoul, a Jacobite in 1745. [JNE.2.9]

CUMING, LACHLAN, in Demerara, a sasine, 24 January 1799. [NRS.RS.Elgin and Forres.494]

CUMMING, ROBERT, in the Raws of Banff, was appointed the Constable of Banff on 7 April 1741. [RB.409]

THE PEOPLE OF MORAY, BANFF, AND NAIRN, 1700-1799

CUMMING, ROBERT, a farmer in Solach of Dollas, was admitted as a burgess of Elgin in 1774. [EBR]

CUMING, THOMAS, in Demerara, a sasine, 3 June 1799. [NRS.RS.Elgin and Forres.508]; in Elgin, late from Demerara, testament, 19 May 1813. [NRS]

CUMING, WILLIAM, master of the Music school in Elgin and session clerk there from 1696. [RE.2.409]

CUMMING, WILLIAM, son of David Cumming of Presley, a sasine, 6 March 1716. [NRS.RS28.108.435]

DALRYMPLE, Sir DAVID, was admitted as a burgess of Elgin in 1763. [EBR]

DAVIDSON, JAMES, born 1732, a servant of Gordon of Carnousie, a Jacobite in 1745. [JNE.2.9]

DAVIDSON, JAMES, a mason, was admitted as a burgess of Elgin on 21 September 1765. [EBR]

DAVIDSON, JOHN, in the Mill of Towie, was appointed the Constable of Fordyce on 7 April 1741. [RB.409]

DAVIDSON, PETER, born 1789 in Findhorn, Moray, settled in Bhaugulpore, India, died in Calcutta, India, on 29 July 1821. [South Park gravestone, Calcutta]

DAVIDSON, ROBERT, born 1786, son of Robert Davidson and his wife Isabella in Findhorn, Moray, died in Calcutta, India, on 20 August 1841. [New Burial Ground gravestone, Circular Road, Calcutta.]

DAVIDSON, ROBERT, in Findhorn, 1802. [NRS.GD248.366.11]

DAVIDSON, WILLIAM, in Forres, 1800. [NRS.CS228.B11.46]

DAVIE, JEAN, widow of William Sym a merchant bailie of Banff, testament, 5 July 1750, Comm. Aberdeen. [NRS]

# THE PEOPLE OF MORAY, BANFF, AND NAIRN, 1700-1799

DAWSON, JAMES, a wright in Kinminity, Banffshire, a Jacobite in 1745. [JNE.2.10]

DAWSON, WILLIAM, a merchant in Forres, papers, 1719-1727. [NRS.GD44.51.455/2]

DEANS, ANDREW, a labourer at the Hill of Tillycairn, Clunie, a Jacobite in 1745. [JNE.2.10]

DENOON, ALEXANDER, a weaver, was admitted as a burgess of Elgin in 1770. [EBR]

DICK, ALEXANDER, a church elder in Elgin in 1709. [RE.2.328]

DICK, ALEXANDER, a glover in Elgin, dead by 1722. [RE.2.331]

DICK, ANDREW, convenor of Elgin, a Jacobite in 1715. [RE.2.379]

DICK, ROBERT, a wheelwright, was admitted as a burgess of Elgin on 21 September 1765. [EBR]

DICK, WILLIAM, master of the Three Friends of Burghead trading with Inverness, 1806. [NRS.E504.5.1]

DICKIE, MARGARET, from Bellie, Banffshire, a Jacobite imprisoned at Lancaster, England, released in 1747. [JNE.2.10]

DICKSON, JANET, spinning mistress in Elgin from 1733. [RE.2.411]

DINGWALL, JOHN, born 1745 in Duthil, son of Alexander Dingwall in Knockelgranish, emigrated to America, possibly aboard the John and Elizabeth in 1775, a Loyalist in 1776, moved to Riviere aux Raisins, Glengarry, Canada, father of Ann and Sophia. [DF][TNA.AO12.29.177]

DONALD, JAMES, servant to Alexander Shaw a merchant, was admitted as a burgess of Elgin in 1748. [EBR]

DONALDSON, ALEXANDER, born 1707, a labourer in Banff, a Jacobite who was captured and transported to the colonies in 1747. [JNE.2.10]

DONALDSON, JAMES, a merchant in Elgin, a sasine, 26 March 1711. [NRS.RS16.99.304]

DONALDSON, JAMES, born 1722, servant to Hay of Rannes, Banffshire, a Jacobite transported to the colonies in 1747. [JNE.2.10]

DONALDSON, JOHN, a bailie of Elgin, a sasine, 25 April 1706, [NRS.RS16.89.61]

DONALDSON, JOHN, a writer in Banff, a Jacobite in 1715. [JNE.9]

DONALDSON, JOHN, a merchant in Elgin, a charter, 15 February 1731. [NRS.RH8.481]

DONALDSON, ROBERT, Writer to the Signet, Sheriff Clerk of Nairn, a process of slander, August 1786. [NRS.CC8.6.748]

DONALDSON, WILLIAM, a smith in Elgin, was admitted as a burgess of Elgin in 1753. [EBR]; a pocket account book, 1761-1777. [NRS.CS96.4220]

DONALDSON, WILLIAM, from Carolina, was admitted as a burgess of Elgin in 1776. [EBR]

DOUCATT, ROBERT, a skipper from Findhorn, an assessor of the Scots Court in Veere, Zealand, in 1719, [NRS.RH11.2]

DOUGALL, WILLIAM, minister at Birnie from 1709 until 1721. [F.6.379]

DOUGLAS, JOHN, was appointed beadle and kirk officer of Elgin in 1750. [RE.2.340]

DOUGLAS, JOHN, a smith, was admitted as a burgess of Elgin in 1753. [EBR]

DOUGLAS, ROBERT, son of baillie William Douglas, was admitted as a burgess of Elgin in 1705. [EBR]

DOUGLAS, PATRICK, from Banffshire, a Jacobite, of the Carlisle garrison in 1746. [JNE.2.10]

DOUGLAS, SAMUEL, Excise supervisor in Forres, a Jacobite in 1745, killed. [JNE.2.10]

DRUM, ALEXANDER, a seaman in Gardenstown, later in Portsoy, testament, 1812, Comm. Aberdeen. [NRS]

DRUM, ……, was admitted as a burgess of Elgin on 7 August 1731. [EBR]

DUFF, ALEXANDER, town clerk of Elgin, versus Eliza Anglin Mackintosh, his spouse, daughter of Dr James Mackintosh in Jamaica, who married on 22 August 1776. Process of Adherance, 5 September 1781. [NRS.CC8.6.639]

DUFF, HUGH ROBERT, of Muirtown, married Sarah Louisa Forbes, daughter of Arthur Forbes of Culloden, at Culloden House on 26 July 1798. [SM.XL.575]

DUFF, JAMES, son of Provost John Duff, was admitted as a burgess of Elgin in 1750. [EBR]

DUFF, JAMES, born in 1741, a merchant in Madeira, was admitted as a burgess of Banff in 1779. [BBR]; died 1 April 1812. [Banff gravestone]

DUFF, JAMES, son of William Duff of Cromby, merchant in Cadiz, Spain, in 1783. [NRS. Services of Heirs]

DUFF, JANET, wife of James Grant of Grant, heir to her father Alexander Duff of Hatton, re lands in Banffshire, 21 July 1766. [NRS.S/H]

DUFF, JOHN, son of Patrick Duff of Craigston, was admitted as a burgess of Elgin in 1709. [EBR]

DUFF, JOHN, a baker in Banff, a Jacobite in 1745. [JNE.2.11]

DUFF, JOHN, son of Provost John Duff, was admitted as a burgess of Elgin in 1750. [EBR]

DUFF, JOHN, a merchant, Provost of Elgin. From 1771 to 1774, 1775 to 1778, 1779 to 1782. 1785 to 1788, 1791 to 1792. [RE.2.477]

DUFF, MARGARET, youngest daughter of William Duff of Whitehill the Provost of Banff, testament, 13 March 1742, Comm. Aberdeen. [NRS]

DUFF, PATRICK, heir to his father Robert Duff minister at Aberlour. 30 April 1750. [NRS.S/H]

DUFF, PATRICK, a Captain of Artillery, Honourable East India Company Service, Bengal, was admitted as a burgess of Banff in 1774. [BBR]; a Colonel in the HEICS, a sasine, 1790. [NRS.RS.Banff.232]

DUFF, PATRICK, son of Patrick Duff the town clerk, was admitted as a burgess of Elgin in 1775. [EBR]

DUFF, ROBERT, son of Alexander Duff in Craignoch, was admitted as a burgess of Elgin in 1711. [EBR]

DUFF, ROBERT, merchant in Banff, son of Thomas Duff a merchant there, testament, 7 April 1748, Comm. Aberdeen. [NRS]

DUFF, SYMON, a tobacconist in Elgin, heir to his brother Henry Duff a burgess of Inverness, 14 March 1750. [NRS.S/H]

DUFF, THOMAS, a skipper from Banff, an assessor of the Scots Court in Veere, Zealand, in 1735-1738. [NRS.RH11.2];

DUFF, WILLIAM, of Dipple, sasines, 18 January 1703, 10 February 1708, 14 December 1713, and 14 December 1716. [NRS.RS16.82.279; RS28.94.66; RS28.104.383; RS16.109.10]

DUFF, WILLIAM, of Dipple, later of Braco, sasine, 16 June 1719. [NRS.RS28.114.125]; a Jacobite in 1715. [JNE.9]

DUFF, WILLIAM, of Bracco, a Justice of the Peace of Banffshire in 1724. [RB.401]

DUFF, WILLIAM, from Banffshire, a member of the Scots Charitable Society of Boston, Massachusetts, in 1760. [NEHGS/SCS]

DUFF, WILLIAM, in St George's, Grenada, was admitted as a burgess of Banff in 1797. [BBR]

DUFF, ……., in Hillocks, was admitted as a burgess of Elgin in 1784. [EBR]

DUFFUS, ALEXANDER, a messenger in Fochabers, a Jacobite in 1745. [JNE.2.11]

DUFFUS, ISOBELL, widow of William Proctor, late in Rothes, testament, 6 December 1751, Comm. Aberdeen. [NRS]

DUNBAR, ALEXANDER, in Forres, 25 April 1702. [NRS.GD110.1248]

DUNBAR, ALEXANDER, of Moy, sasines, 10 February 1708, and 14 February 1713. [NRS.RS28.94.66; RS28.104.383]

DUNBAR, ARCHIBALD, of Thounderton, Provost of Elgin, a Jacobite in 1715. [RE.2.379]

DUNBAR, ELIZABETH, widow of Sir Robert Gordon of Gordonstoun, a sasine, 24 January 1705. [NRS.RS28.86.166]

DUNBAR, ELIZABETH, daughter of William Dunbar a merchant in Forres, heir to her brother William Dunbar a merchant in London, 7 October 1796. [NRS.S/H]

DUNBAR, JAMES, born 1730, a labourer from Moray, a Jacobite in 1745. [JNE.2.11]

DUNBAR, JAMES, a tailor, was admitted as a burgess of Elgin in 1769. [EBR]

DUNBAR, JAMES, a tailor, was admitted as a burgess of Elgin in 1774. [EBR]

DUNBAR, JOHN, sheriff depute of Moray, sasines, 7 December 1716. [NRS.RS28.110.147; RS28.110.156]

DUNBAR, ROBERT, a physician in Banff, testament, 28 July 1772, Comm. Aberdeen. [NRS]

DUNBAR, STEVEN, son of Walter Dunbar in Forres, died in Jamaica in September 1780. [SM.42.617]

DUNBAR, WILLIAM, born 13 November 1740, son of Robert Dunbar in Dyke, Forres, a member of the Scots Charitable Society of Boston, Massachusetts, in 1766. [NEHGS/SCS]

DUNBAR, Sir WILLIAM, eldest son of Sir James Dunbar and his wife Margaret Baird, a Jacobite in 1745, died in Banff on 28 January 1786. [JNE.2.11]

DUNBAR, WILLIAM, born in the parish of Moy and Culbin, son of Reverend Robert Dunbar of Ballinspink, [1707-1782], and his wife Jean Miller [died 1788], sometime in Grenada, died in London. [F.6.413]

DUNBAR, WILLIAM, born 1749 in Moray, son of Sir Archibald Dunbar of Thunderston, Elgin, [1693-1769]. And his wife Anne Bain. emigrated to Philadelphia, Pennsylvania, in 1771, a trader there, and later at Fort Pitt, afterwards a planter in Florida, in Louisiana, and finally at Natchez, Adams County, Mississippi by 1773. He died in 1810. [Dunbar papers, University of North Carolina]

DUNCAN, ALEXANDER, schoolmaster of Elgin from 1695. [RE.2.409]

DUNCAN, ALEXANDER, skipper in Portsoy, testament, 24 May 1756, Comm. Aberdeen. [NRS]

DUNCAN, ALEXANDER, a watchmaker, was admitted as a burgess of Elgin in 1785. [EBR]

DUNCAN, GEORGE, a servant from Fochabers, a Jacobite in 1745. [JNE.2.11]

DUNCAN, JOHN, in Blairhall, was admitted as a burgess of Elgin in 1750. [EBR]

DUNCAN, JOHN, a merchant in Alves, was admitted as a burgess of Elgin in 1781. [EBR]

DUNCAN, WILLIAM, eldest son of John Duncan a hirer in Elgin, a corporal in the King's Regiment of Foot, was admitted as a burgess of Elgin in 1749. [EBR]

DUNCANSON, ROBERT, a merchant in Fredericksburg, Virginia, died there in 1764, brother of Thomas Duncanson, a surgeon in Forres, Moray. [Spotsylvania Deed Book G., 7 July 1764, Virginia]

DUNLOP, DAVID, was educated at Edinburgh University, minister at Birnie from 1721 until his death on 29 May 1742. [F.6.379]

DUNNON, JOHN, from Banff, a Jacobite in 1745. [JNE.2.12]

EDINSON, WILLIAM, from Banffshire, a Jacobite in 1745. [JNE.2.12]

ELDER, JAMES, a merchant in Banff, testament, 18 July 1754, Comm. Aberdeen. [NRS]

ELLIS, ALEXANDER, sr., in Peterhead, was admitted as a burgess of Elgin in 1783. [EBR]

ELLIS, ALEXANDER, jr., in Peterhead, was admitted as a burgess of Elgin in 1783. [EBR]

ELLIS, WILLIAM, in Banff, testament, 19 April 1794, Comm. Aberdeen. [NRS]

ELPHINSTONE, ROBIN, a goldsmith in Forres, a bond, around 1710. [NRS.GD133.186]

ERSKINE, MARIA, born on 9 November 1791 in the East Indies, died in Banff on 25 May 1807. [Banff gravestone]

FAIRFIELD, ......, was admitted as a burgess of Elgin on 7 August 1731. [EBR]

FALCONER, COLIN, master of the Pretty Betsey of Portsoy trading between Aberdeen, Newcastle, England, and Veere, Zealand, in 1743. [NRS.E504.1.1]

FALCONER, JAMES, master of the Mary of Nairn trading between Oporto, Portugal, and Inverness in 1742. [NRS.E504.17.1]

FALCONER, JOHN, was admitted as a burgess of Elgin in 1782. [EBR]

FALCONER, PATRICK, born 1775, son of William Falconer, a farmer in Kinnermany, [1720-1793] and his wife Anna Rose, [1743-1821], a merchant in New York, died in 1837. [Inveraven gravestone]

FALCONER, ROBERT, a smith in the College of Elgin, was admitted as a burgess of Elgin in 1761. [EBR]

FALCONER, ROBERT, born 1782, son of William Falconer, a farmer in Kinnermany, [1720-1793] and his wife Anna Rose, [1743-1821], a merchant in New York, died in 1851. [Inveraven gravestone]

FALCONER, WILLIAM, born 1763, son of William Falconer, a farmer in Kinnermany, [1720-1793] and his wife Anna Rose, [1743-1821], a merchant in New York, died in 1818. [Inveraven gravestone]

FALCONER, WILLIAM FYER, born 1807, son of Captain D. Falconer and his wife Catherine, died in Grenada on 30 May 1844. [Rothes gravestone]

FARQUHAR, JAMES, a merchant in Portsoy, testaments, 1742/1748, Comm. Aberdeen. [NRS]

FARQUHAR, JAMES, a farmer in Burnside, Banff, a Jacobite in 1745. [JNE.2.12]

FARQUHAR, JOHN, a merchant in Portsoy, heir to his father James Farquhar a merchant there, 22 July 1769, 22 July 1769. [NRS.S/H]

FARQUHAR, MARGARET, spouse of Alexander Nicolson a tailor in Forres, a sasine, 7 December 1716. [NRS.RS28.110.151]

FARQUHAR, Colonel, was admitted as a burgess of Elgin on 1 October 1731. [EBR]

FARQUHARSON, CHARLES, born 1779, son of James Farquharson and his wife Ann Stuart, in Ballinstruan, Kirkmichael, died in Baltimore, Maryland, on 2 June 1860. [Inveravon Downan gravestone]

FARQUHARSON, JOHN, son of James Farquharson of Coldrach, died in Jamaica on 14 October 1808. [SM.71.237]

FARQUHARSON, ROBERT, born 1777, son of James Farquharson and his wife Ann Stuart, in Ballinstruan, Kirkmichael, died in Nashville, Tennessee, on 28 June 1856. [Inveravon Downan gravestone]

FARQUHARSON, WILLIAM, from Banffshire, a Jacobite in 1745. [JNE.2.15]

FERGUSON, ALEXANDER, master of the William of Portsoy in 1747. [NRS.E504.1.2]; master of the James and Ann of Portsoy trading with Lisbon, Portugal, in 1749. [NRS.E504.1.3]

FERGUSON, JAMES, from Tomintoul, a Jacobite in 1745. [JNE.2.15]

FERGUSON, JOHN, a merchant in Edinburgh, versus Margaret Fimister, his spouse, relict of Alexander Roust a music master in Elgin, who married in Edinburgh on 20 September 1762. Process of Declarator of Marriage. [NRS.CC8.6.419]

FERRIER, JOHN, a ship's carpenter from Banff, then in Aberdeen, testament, 28 April 1794, Comm. Aberdeen. [NRS]

FIFE, WILLIAM, a farmer in Down, Banff, a Jacobite in 1745. [JNE.2.15]

FINDLATOR, ALEXANDER STEPHEN, son of James Findlator in Jamaica, was admitted as a burgess of Banff in 1777. [BBR]

FINDLAY, JAMES, master of the James and Ann of Portsoy trading between Rotterdam, Zealand, and Inverness in 1742. [NRS.E504.17.1]

FINDLAY, WILLIAM, was admitted as a burgess of Elgin in 1782. [EBR]

FINLAY, ALEXANDER, a weaver in Elgin, a Jacobite in 1745. [JNE.2.15]

FINLAY, JAMES, a Jacobite in 1715. [RE.2.379]

FINNY, JAMES, master of the Triton of Banff trading between Bergen, Norway, and Aberdeen in 1744. [NRS.E504.1.1]

FINNIE, JOHN, a skipper in Macduff, testament, 1823, Comm. Aberdeen. [NRS]

FINNIE, MARGARET, widow of James Gray sr. a shoemaker in Banff, testaments, 1722 and 1753. Comm. Aberdeen. [NRS]

FLEMING, JAMES, from Croughly near Tomintoul, a Jacobite in 1745. [JNE.2.15]

FLEMING, JOHN, from Findran, Banffshire, a Jacobite in 1745. [JNE.2.15]

FORBES, ALEXANDER, a church elder in Elgin in 1709. [RE.2.328]

FORBES, ALEXANDER, a tidewaiter at Portknockie, testament, 14 February 1740, Comm. Aberdeen. [NRS]

FORBES, ALEXANDER, a labourer from Banff, a Jacobite in the Carlisle garrison in 1746. [JNE.2.16]

FORBES, CHARLES, a Captain of the $60^{th}$ Regiment of Foot, died at Ticonderoga, New York, in 1758. [Banff gravestone]

FORBES, ELIZABETH, widow of George Philp a merchant in Banff, heir to her father Captain George Forbes of Boyndlie who died in June 1740, 4 March 1772. [NAS.S/H]

FORBES, GEORGE, son of Arthur Forbes of Carnousie, a soldier bound for Holland in 1739. [NRS.RH15.1.169-176]

FORBES, JOHN, from Banffshire, was educated at Marischal College in Aberdeen in 1733, an Episcopalian minister in New Jersey from 1733 until his death in 1736. [CCMC]

FORBES, JOHN, a merchant in Candelmore, Banffshire, a Jacobite in 1745. [JNE.2.16]

FORBES, Sir ROBERT, of Auchinhoove, a sasine, Banff, 1704. [NRS.RS3.85.191]

FORBES, ROBERT, a tenant farmer near Banff in 1745. [JNE.2.16]

FORBES, THOMAS, a merchant in Elgin, a 'papist' in 1735. [RE.2.383]

FORBES, WILLIAM, a writer in Edinburgh, was admitted as a burgess of Elgin in 1732. [EBR]

FORBES, WILLIAM, a Jacobite from Banff, transported to the colonies in 1746. [JNE.2.17]

FORBES, WILLIAM, a farmer at Wester Gauldwell, Boharm, a Jacobite in 1745. [JNE.2.17]

FORBES, WILLIAM, born 1727, a husbandman in Fochaber, a Jacobite transported to the colonies in 1747. [JNE.2.17]

FORBES, Dr, was admitted as a burgess of Elgin in 1771. [EBR]

FORD, HENRY, a Royal Navy surgeon in Nairn, testament, 1808, Comm. Moray. [NRS]

FORDYCE, ALEXANDER, minister at Raffuird, father of Anna, a sasine, Elgin and Forres, 1716. [NRS.RS3.109.273]

FORDYCE, BARBARA, spouse of George Hay a merchant in Buckie, a sasine, 28 August 1716. [NRS.RS28.109.298]

FORDYCE, SARA, spouse of Sir Francis Grant of Cullen, a sasine, 28 August 1716. [NRS.RS28.109.298]

FORREST, JOHN, master of the <u>Neptune of Banff</u> trading between Aberdeen, Bergen, Norway, Trontheim, Norway, and Gothenburg, Sweden, in 1743. [NRS.E504.1.1]

FORSYTH, ALEXANDER, in Forres, 1772, accounts. [NRS.GD248.533.2/19]

FORSYTH, GEORGE, a merchant, was admitted as a burgess of Elgin in 1752. [EBR]

FORSYTH, GEORGE, a smith, was admitted as a burgess of Elgin in 1757. [EBR]

FORSYTH, ISAAC, a merchant, was admitted as a burgess of Elgin in 1788. [EBR]

FORSYTH, JAMES, a glazier in Elgin, in 1702. [RE.2.325]

FORSYTH, JAMES, town officer of Forres, a Jacobite in 1745. [JNE.2.17]

FOTHERINGHAM, Dr CHARLES, a physician in Banff, testament, 14 May 1747, Comm. Aberdeen. [NRS]

FRASER, ALEXANDER, born 1725, from Moray, a Jacobite transported to Barbados in 1747. [JNE.2.17]

FRASER, ALEXANDER or ANGUS, brother of William Fraser of Belnain, was in Mexico during the 1760s. [NRS.NRAS.OOO2]

FRASER, ALEXANDER, born 26 September 1781, son of Alexander Fraser, a merchant in Forres, and his wife Jane Warden, an officer in the Bengal Army from 1824 until his death in Benares, India, on 20 July 1843. [BA.2.215]

FRASER, DAVID, from Banffshire, a Jacobite who was transported to the colonies in 1747. [JNE.2.17]

FRASER, DONALD, a Jacobite in Portsoy in 1745. [JNE.2.17]

FRASER, HUGH, born in Moray during 1769, Professor of Divinity in Georgetown, South Carolina, naturalised in South Carolina on 21 February 1817. [NARA.M1183]

FRASER, JAMES, from Upper Cults, Banffshire, a Jacobite in 1745. [JNE.2.17]

FRASER, JAMES, a shoemaker, was admitted as a burgess of Elgin in 1774. [EBR]

FRASER, JAMES, heir to his father John Fraser a feuar in Fochabers, 26 June 1794. [NRS.S/H]

FRASER, JOHN, master of the White Swan of Portsoy trading with Collysound, Norway, in 1751-1752. [NRS.E504.1.4]

FRASER, JOHN, a stay-maker, was admitted as a burgess of Elgin in 1775. [EBR]

FRASER, ROBERT, was admitted as a burgess of Elgin in 1782. [EBR]

FRASER, ROBERT WARDEN, born 3 January 1806 in Forres, son of Alexander Fraser, a merchant, [died 27 October 1816], and his wife Jean Warden, a Captain of the $45^{th}$ Bengal Native Infantry of the Bengal Army from 1821 to 1853, died in Edinburgh on 30 June 1876. [BA.2.220][NRS.Services of Heirs, 1851]

FRASER, THOMAS, from Banff, a Jacobite imprisoned in Stirling in 1746. [JNE.2.17]

FRASER, WILLIAM, a butcher in Whitewreath, was admitted as a burgess of Elgin in 1758. [EBR]

FRASER, WILLIAM, was admitted as a burgess of Elgin in 1759. [EBR]

FRASER, WILLIAM, was admitted as a burgess of Elgin in 1782. [EBR]

FRASER, WILLIAM TULLOCH, son of Alexander Fraser, a merchant in Forres, [died 27 October 1816], and his wife Jean Warden, a merchant in Calcutta, India, in 1851. [NRS.Services of Heirs]

FRIGGE, ANDREW, servant to Alexander Gray a wheelwright, was admitted as a burgess of Elgin on 21 September 1765. [EBR]

FRIGG, ELIZABETH, servant in Barnhill, rebuked for breaking the Sabbath, in 1762, [RE.2.344]

FYFE, DAVID, in Jamaica, was admitted as a burgess of Banff in 1775. [BBR]

GAIRDEN, GEORGE, at Blairshinnoch, was appointed the Constable of Banff on 7 April 1741. [RB.409]

GAIRDYN, GEORGE, an attorney in St Mary's, Jamaica, was admitted as a burgess of Banff in 1784. [BBR]

GAIRNS, ROBERT, minister in St Fergus, Banffshire, 1757. [NRS.E326.1.17]

GAMATSGAIRN, PETER, from Banff, a Jacobite in 1745. [JNE.2.18]

GARDEN, ALEXANDER, in Gamry, 1748. [NRS.E326.1.17]

GARDEN, ANN, widow of James Innes the provost and a merchant in Banff, testament, 22 February 1772, Comm. Aberdeen. [NRS]

GARDEN, GEORGE, a merchant, provost, and bailie of Banff, testaments, 1740/1745, Comm. Aberdeen. [NRS]

GARDEN, JOHN, a vagabond in Banff Tolbooth, released to enrol in Lieutenant General Collier's Regiment of the Scots Brigade in the service of Holland, on 4 May 1724. [RB.401]

GARDINER, JAMES, born 1760, late in Jamaica, died in Banff on 22 May 1820, husband of Margaret Aven, born 1762, died 1831. [Banff gravestone]; testament 30 October 1830. [NRS.CC1.6.W993]

GARDYNE, SAMUEL, from Charleston, South Carolina, was admitted as a burgess of Banff in 1785. [BBR]

GATHERER, GEORGE, a mason in Lossiemouth, was admitted as a burgess of Elgin in 1761. [EBR]

GATHERER, JOHN, a weaver, was admitted as a burgess of Elgin in 1760. [EBR]

GATT, ALEXANDER, a servant to Arthur Gordon of Carnousie, Banff, a Jacobite in 1745. [JNE.2.18]

GATT, JAMES, born in Cullen in 1699, educated at King's College, Aberdeen, a Jacobite in 1715, later a minister at Gretna, died 31 October 1787. [JNE.17]

GAULD, JOHN, from Achnagra in the Braes of Glenlivet, a Jacobite in 1745. [JNE.2.18]

GAULD, THOMAS, from Achlanie, Tomintoul, a Jacobite in 1745. [JNE.2.18]

GEDDES, GEORGE, chamberlain to the Laird of Dipple, was admitted as a burgess of Elgin in 1706. [EBR]

THE PEOPLE OF MORAY, BANFF, AND NAIRN, 1700-1799

GEDDES, JAMES, a merchant in Elgin, husband of Margaret Innes, parents of Marjorie Geddes, a declaration, 29 August 1730. [SRS.Barony of Innes Writs.386/10]

GEDDES, JAMES, a merchant in Gardenston, testament, 7 July 1787, Comm. Aberdeen. [NRS]

GEDDES, JOHN, son of William Geddes minister at Urquhart, a sasine in Moray 1710. [NRS.RS29.5.210]

GEDDES, JOHN, born 1753, died 1817, husband of Helen Todd, born 1771, died 1837, parents of George Geddes, born 1808, died in Jamaica on 24 May 1864. [Bellie gravestone]

GEDDES, JOHN, born 1788, son of John Geddes and his wife Margaret Anderson, an assistant surgeon of the 54$^{th}$ Regiment, died in Jamaica in November 1808. [Bellie gravestone]

GEDDES, WILLIAM, son of Andrew Geddes of Essil, was admitted as a burgess of Elgin in 1707. [EBR]

GEDDES, WILLIAM, a weaver, was admitted as a burgess of Elgin in 1769. [EBR]

GEDLIE, ROBERT, a weaver, was admitted as a burgess of Elgin in 1760. [EBR]

GELLIE, ALEXANDER, minister at Fordyce, sasines, 16 June 1704, and 1 August 1719. [NRS.RS16.85.77; RS28.114.258]

GELLIE, JAMES, son of the minister at Fordyce, sasine, 1 August 1719. [NRS.RS28.114.258]

GELLIE, MARGARET, daughter of the minister of Fordyce, spouse of William Leslie, son of John Leslie of Bardonsyde, a sasine, 1 August 1719. [NRS.RS28.114.258]

GIBB, ANDREW, tenant in Durn, Banffshire, a Jacobite in 1745. [JNE.2.18]

GIBENACH, THOMAS, from Scalan, Banffshire, a Jacobite in 1745. [JNE.2.18]

GILBERT, ROBERT, a tailor, was admitted as a burgess of Elgin in 1776. [EBR]

GILBERT, WILLIAM, a servant from Cushnie, Banffshire, a Jacobite in 1745. [JNE.2.18]

GILCHRIST, JAMES, minister of Alves, from 1697 until 1700. [F.6.376]

GILL, ALEXANDER, a servant in Cushnie, Banffshire, a Jacobite in 1745. [JNE.2.18]

GILL, JAMES, master of the Katty of Banff trading with Leith in July 1806. [NRS.E504.5.1]

GILL, PETER, master of the William of Portsoy trading with Bergen, and Kristiansand, Norway, also Bo'ness in 1751-1752. [NRS.E504.1.3/4]

GILLIARD, JOHN, in Charleston, South Carolina, was admitted as a burgess of Banff in 1785. [BBR]

GILZEAN, JOHN, a farmer, was admitted as a burgess of Elgin in 1796. [EBR]

GILZEAN, THOMAS, clerk to Patrick Duff, was admitted as a burgess of Elgin in 1775. [EBR]

GLASS, JAMES, a wigmaker, was admitted as a burgess of Elgin in 1705. [EBR]

GLASS, JAMES, a merchant in Nairn, a bond, 9 December 1730. [NRS.CC2.13.7.3]

GOODBRAND, ALEXANDER, born 1717, a carpenter in Banff, a Jacobite prisoner bound for the Leeward Islands, liberated by the French and landed on Martinique in 1747. [JNE.2.18]

GOODBRAND, JOHN, a wright in Cullen, a Jacobite in 1745. [JNE.2.19]

THE PEOPLE OF MORAY, BANFF, AND NAIRN, 1700-1799

GOODBRAND, WALTER, a feuar in Portsoy, heir to his cousin Ann Goodbrand daughter of Alexander Goodbrand in Portsoy, 14 November 1775, and to his father John Goodbrand a feuar there, 15 April 1777. [NRS.S/H]

GORDON, ALEXANDER, son of James Gordon the minister at Rothiemay, a sasine, Banff, 1705. [NRS.RS3.87.370]

GORDON, ALEXANDER, of Auchyndochie, a sasine, Banff, 1705. [NRS.RS3.87.298]

GORDON, ALEXANDER, of Camdell, a sasine, Banff, 1711. [NRS.RS3.100.306]

GORDON, ALEXANDER, in Parkmore, a sasine, Elgin and Forres, 1713. [NRS.RS3.103.75]

GORDON, ALEXANDER, a Roman Catholic priest, son of John Gordon of Barrack, a Jacobite in 1745, died in Inverness jail in 1746. [JNE.2.19]

GORDON, ALEXANDER, of Kinmundy, a sasine, Banff, 1718. [NRS.RS3.113.203]

GORDON, ALEXANDER, of Pitlurg, a sasine, 1718, Banff. [NRS.RS3.113.203]

GORDON, ALEXANDER, from Refreish, Banffshire, a Jacobite in 1745. [JNE.2.19]

GORDON, ALEXANDER, of Letterfourie, born 1715, a farmer in Pattenbringan, Banff, a Jacobite in 1745, moved to Madeira, died 16 January 1797. [JNE.2.19]

GORDON, ALEXANDER, of Binhall, schoolmaster of Cairnie in 1742, a Jacobite in 1745. [JNE.2.19]

GORDON, ALEXANDER, born 30 January 1750, son of Reverend George Gordon and his wife Agnes Brodie in Alves, died in India. [F.6.376]

THE PEOPLE OF MORAY, BANFF, AND NAIRN, 1700-1799

GORDON, ALEXANDER, a merchant in St Martins, France, a sasine in Elgin, 1740. [NRS.RS29.6.468]

GORDON, ALEXANDER, in Rathven, 1748. [NRS.E326.1.17]

GORDON, ALEXANDER, born 1755, son of Reverend Harry Gordon [1730-1764] and his wife Sarabella Morrison, in Fordyce, a planter in Tobago, died 1781. [F.6.434; F.5.534]

GORDON, ALEXANDER, of Cairnfield, Raffan, 1757. [NRS.E326.1.17]

GORDON, ARTHUR, of Carnousie, a Jacobite in 1745, escaped to France. [JNE.2.19]

GORDON, CATHERINE, spouse of James Gordon the minister at Rothiemay, a sasine, Banff, 1705. [NRS.RS3.87.370]

GORDON, CHARLES, of Glengearock, a sasine, 1708, Banff. [NRS.RS3.94.35]

GORDON, CHARLES, a gentleman in Eldornie, Banff, a Jacobite in 1745. [JNE.2.20]

GORDON, CHARLES, born on 28 January 1777, son of Reverend Lewis Gordon and his wife Elizabeth Logan in Elgin, died aboard the Harriet on the homeward voyage from India. [F.6.391]

GORDON, ELIZABETH, spouse to Alexander Gordon of Cairnfield, Sasines, Banff, 1724. [NRS.RS3.122.370/372]

GORDON, ELSPETH, daughter of Robert Gordon a merchant in Elgin, a sasine, 1727. Elgin. [NRS.RS3.129.409]

GORDON, FRANCIS, of Craig of Auchendoun, a sasine. Banff, 1707. [NRS.RS3.93.412]

GORDON, GEORGE, from Banff, a citizen of Bergen, Norway, in 1700. [SAB]

GORDON, GEORGE, born 1692, educated at Marischal College, Aberdeen, schoolmaster of Rothes from 1710 to 1712, minister of

Boharm from 1717 until 1727, minister of Alves from 1728 until his death on 3 March 1752. Husband of [1] Elizabeth Gordon, parents of Isabel, husband of [2] Agnes Brodie, parents of William, Jean, Mary, Harry, Barbara, George, James, Thomas, David, and Alexander. [F.6.376]

GORDON, GEORGE, of Buckie, a Jacobite in 1715, died 1729, testaments, 1729.1732/1734/1756, Comm. Aberdeen. [NRS][JNE19]

GORDON, Captain GEORGE, of Carnousie, son of Sir George Gordon of Edinglassie, a sasine, Banff, 1724. [NRS.RS3.122.349]

GORDON, GEORGE, from Tomintoul, a Jacobite in 1745, killed in action. [JNE.2.21]

GORDON, GEORGE, from Newtown of Glenlivet, a Jacobite in 1745. [JNE.2.21]

GORDON, GEORGE, of Glenbucket, a Jacobite, fought at Culloden in 1746, died as a doctor in Jamaica. [JNE.2.21]

GORDON, GEORGE, of Nethermuir, a sasine, Elgin and Forres, 1721. [NRS.RS3.118.239]

GORDON, Dr GEORGE, a physician in Banff, testament, 20 September 1733, Comm. Aberdeen. [NRS]

GORDON, GEORGE, in Rathven, 1748. [NRS.E326.1.17]

GORDON, GEORGE, journeyman to John Baron, Deacon of the Shoemakers, was admitted as a burgess of Elgin on 21 September 1765. [EBR]

GORDON, GEORGE, son of Dr William Gordon, a physician in St Croix, Danish West Indies, was admitted as a burgess of Banff in 1767. [BBR]

GORDON, HARRY, a preacher in Forres, a letter of horning, 2 November 1754. [NRS.GD23.5.293]

GORDON, HELEN, in Banff, testament, 2 June 1748, Comm. Aberdeen. [NRS]

GORDON, HELEN, sometime wife to James Innes, later widow of James Alexander a wright in Banff, testament, 11 October 1798, Comm. Aberdeen. [NRS]

GORDON, JAMES, a chapman in Strathbogie, was admitted as a burgess of Elgin in 1699. [EBR]

GORDON, JAMES, minister at Rothiemay, a sasine, 23 August 1705. [NRS.RS16.87.375]

GORDON, JAMES, of Daach, a sasine, Banff, 1715. [NRS.RS3.107.253]

GORDON, JAMES, heir to his brother Archibald Gordon, who died in September 1741, son of Peter Gordon of Ardmeallie, in the lands and barony of Zeuchrie, Banffshire, 5 April 1753. [NRS.S/H]

GORDON, JAMES, born 1719, of Birkenbush, Cullen, a Jacobite in 1745, transported as a prisoner to the colonies in 1747. [JNE.2.21]

GORDON, JAMES, in Rathven, 1748. [NRS.E326.1.17]

GORDON, JAMES, a cooper in Garmouth, a sasine, 1724, Elgin and Forres, 1724. [NRS.RS3.123.269]

GORDON, JAMES, a merchant in Banff, testament, 22 January 1753, Comm. Aberdeen. [NRS]

GORDON, JAMES, a merchant in Portsoy, testament, 8 April 1754, Comm. Aberdeen. [NRS]

GORDON, JAMES, a merchant in Forres, heir to his father James Gordon a merchant there, 17 March 1756. [NRS.S/H]

GORDON, JAMES, of Clashtirum, Raffan, 1757. [NRS.E326.1.17]

GORDON, JAMES, a shoemaker, was admitted as a burgess of Elgin in 1757. [EBR]

GORDON, JAMES, son of Alexander Gordon a merchant, was admitted as a burgess of Elgin in 1762. [EBR]

GORDON, JAMES COSMO, born 13 August 1756, son of John Gordon of Birkenbush, an officer of the Bengal Army from 1781 to 1792, died in 1792. [BA.2.288]

GORDON, JANET, wife of John Duff a merchant in Elgin, heir to her mother Ann Smith, daughter of Henry Smith of Smithfield, and to her grandfather Henry Smith of Smithfield a merchant in Dundee, 8 September 1753. [NRS.S/H]

GORDON, JOHN, factor in Veere, Zealand, was admitted as a burgess of Elgin in 1682. [EBR]

GORDON, JOHN, of Rothiemay, a sasine, 18 January 1712. [NRS.RS16.101.120]

GORDON, JOHN, a merchant in Elgin, a Jacobite in 1715. [RE.2.379]

GORDON, JOHN, of Nether Buckie, the younger, a Lieutenant in the Earl of Orkney's Regiment, a sasine, 1724, Banff. [NRS.RS3.122.375]

GORDON, JOHN, in Belly, Moray, 1748. [NRS.E326.1.17]

GORDON, JOHN, in Fordyce, 1753. [NRS.E326.1.17]

GORDON, JOHN, a writer in Elgin, a missive, 21 June 1764. [SRS.Barony of Innes Writs, 191/2]

GORDON, JOHN, a merchant, was admitted as a burgess of Elgin in 1765. [EBR]

GORDON, ....., of Aberdour, was admitted as a burgess of Elgin in 1787. [EBR]

GORDON, JOHN, born 5 June 1775, son of Reverend Lewis Gordon and his wife Elizabeth Logan in Elgin, died in Calcutta on 7 February 1802. [F.6.391]

THE PEOPLE OF MORAY, BANFF, AND NAIRN, 1700-1799

GORDON, JOHN, born 19 May 1795, son of Reverend William Gordon and his wife Catherine Brodie, a surgeon in Honourable East India Company Service, died in the Persian Gulf on 2 March 1821. [F.6.391]

GORDON, LEWIS, MA, minister of Drainie from 1768 until 1815. Graduated DD from King's College, Aberdeen, on 17 February 1815. [F.6.383]

GORDON, LEWIS, born 19 October 1780, son of Reverend Lewis Gordon and his wife Elizabeth Logan in Elgin, a Lieutenant in Honourable East India Company Service, died in India on 5 December 1801. [F.6.391]

GORDON, MARGARET, sister of George Gordon of Arradowll, a sasine, Banff, 1702. [NRS.RS3.81.159]

GORDON, MARGARET, a 'papist' in Elgin, daughter of James Gordon, a merchant, and his wife Jean Stuart, 5 August 1735. [RE.2.383]

GORDON, MARGARET, widow of …. Cuming in Cullen, testament, 9 August 1753, Comm. Aberdeen. [NRS]

GORDON, Mrs MARY, in Fordyce, 1753. [NRS.E326.1.17]

GORDON, Mrs MARY, in Banff, widow of Thomas Innes of Muiryfold, testament, 17 February 1784, Comm. Aberdeen. [NRS]

GORDON, PATRICK, of Aberlour, 1757. [NRS.E326.1.17]

GORDON, PATRICK, minister in Belly, 1757. [NRS.E326.1.17]

GORDON, Sir ROBERT, of Gordonstoun, sasines, 24 January 1705, 2 January 1706, and 17 January 1715. [NRS.RS28.86.166; RS28.88.228; RS28.106.453]

GORDON, Sir ROBERT, of Gordonstoun, 1757. [NRS.CS271.76.371]

GORDON, ROBERT, a manufacturer in Keith, was admitted as a burgess of Elgin in 1759. [EBR]

GORDON, THOMAS, of Spynie, was admitted as a burgess of Elgin in 1787. [EBR]

GORDON, WALTER, tidesman at Banff, testament, 10 March 1725, Comm. Aberdeen. [NRS]

GORDON, WILLIAM, a factor in Veere, Zealand, was admitted as a burgess of Elgin in 1686. [EBR]

GORDON, WILLIAM, a merchant in Banff, testaments, 1742/1748, Comm. Aberdeen. [NRS]

GORDON, WILLIAM, in Forres, letters, 1733 – 1743. [NRS.GD23.6.108]

GORDON, WILLIAM, an Admiral of the Royal Navy, in Banff, testament, 27 August 1774, Comm. Aberdeen. [NRS]

GORDON, WILLIAM, born 1780, settled in Tobago, died in Elgin in 1832. [Rothes Dundurcas gravestone]

GRANT, A., in Edinburgh, was admitted as a burgess of Elgin in 1784. [EBR]

GRANT, ALEXANDER, of Conrack, a sasine, Elgin and Forres, 1713. [NRS.RS3.103.75]

GRANT, ALEXANDER, in Cullen, 1748. [NRS.E326.1.17]

GRANT, ALEXANDER, in Keith, 1757. [NRS.E326.1.17]

GRANT, ALEXANDER, baptised 7 August 1793 in Moray, son of Robert Grant of Wester Elchies, an officer of the Bengal Army from 1809 to 1829, died in Edinburgh on 13 August 1835. [BA.2.311]

GRANT, ANNA, born 1 August 1762, daughter of Reverend John Grant and his wife Anna Grant in Elgin, wife of James Brice the collector of Revenue in Washington, Pennsylvania, later in Pittsburgh. [F.6.394]

GRANT, CHARLES, was admitted as a burgess of Elgin in 1784. [EBR]

GRANT, COLQUHOUN, was admitted as a burgess of Forres on 28 September 1779. [NRS.GD1.79.12]

GRANT, DUNCAN, a baillie and merchant in Forres, papers, 1766-1767. [NRS.GD248.51/1]

GRANT, Sir FRANCIS, of Cullen, sasines, 28 August 1716, 30 April 1717, and 27 November 1705. [NRS.RS28.109.298; RS16.110; RS16.110.418.]

GRANT, GEORGE, late in Jamaica, a sasine, 1796. [NRS.RS.Elgin and Forres.410]

GRANT, HUMPHREY, a merchant in F accounts, 1768-1776; in Forres, a letter, 24 November 1788. [NRS.GD248.243.9/14; GD248.533.4.67]

GRANT, ISAAC, was admitted as a burgess of Elgin in 1784. [EBR]

GRANT, JAMES, a soldier from Elgin, married Ann Lindsay, from Dundee, in Schiedam, the Netherlands, on 19 December 1637. [Schiedam Marriage Register]

GRANT, JAMES, from Strathspey, a student at Utrecht University in the Netherlands from 1699 to 1702. [Royal College of Physicians of Edinburgh]

GRANT, JAMES, a servant to John Elphinstone, was admitted as a burgess of Elgin in 1709. [EBR]

GRANT, Sir JAMES, of Grant, a sasine, Banff, 1733. [NRS.RS3.143.149]

GRANT, JAMES, a tack of lands in Cromdale, 9 October 1751. [NRS.GD248.533.3/55]

GRANT, JAMES, of Carron, Aberlour, 1757. [NRS.E326.1.17]

GRANT, Colonel JAMES, Governor of East Florida, a sasine, 1770. [NRS.RS29.8.202]

GRANT, JAMES, factor of Strathspey, correspondence, 1795-1799. [NRS.GD248.366.3-10]

THE PEOPLE OF MORAY, BANFF, AND NAIRN, 1700-1799

GRANT, JAMES, born 1783, son of John Grant, a farmer in Croft, and his wife Jean Fraser, a wright in North Carolina, died in 1828. [Cromdale gravestone]

GRANT, JAMES THOMAS, in the East Indies, son of Sir James Grant of Grant, a sasine, 1803. [NRS.RS29.620]

GRANT, JAMES, born 1785 in Lynstock, Grantown, died 20 September 1829. [Scotch Burial Ground gravestone, Calcutta, India]

GRANT, JAMES, factor of Strathspey, correspondence, 1800-1803. [NRS.GD248.366.11]

GRANT, JANET, a 'papist' in Elgin on 5 August 1735. [RE.2.383]

GRANT, JOHN, the younger, of Ballindalloch, a Lieutenant in Lieutenant General Collier's Regiment of the Scots Brigade in the service of Holland, on 4 May 1724. [RB.401]

GRANT, JOHN, in Jamaica, was admitted as a burgess of Banff in 1775. [BBR]; in Jamaica, later in Banff, testament, 1807. [NRS.CC1.6.W329]

GRANT, JAMES, formerly a Captain in Honourable East India Company Service, was admitted as a burgess of Banff in 1778. [BBR]

GRANT, JOHN, born 1713, a weaver in Banff, a Jacobite in 1745, transported in 1747, sold in Oxford, Maryland, on 5 August 1747. [JNE.2.25]

GRANT, JOHN, son of John Grant a merchant in Tomintoul, a Jacobite in 1745. [JNE.2.25]

GRANT, JOHN ROY, from Demickmore, Glenlivet, a Jacobite in 1745. [JNE.2.25]

GRANT, JOHN, in Belly, Moray, 1748. [NRS.E326.1.17]

GRANT, JOHN PETER, of Rothiemurchus, heir to his uncle Patrick Grant of Rothiemurchus, 16 March 1796. [NRS.S/H]

GRANT, Sir LUDOVICK, of Dalvey, heir to his brother Sir Alexander Grant of Dalvey who died in August 1772. [NRS.S/H]

GRANT, LUDOVICK, born 2 August 1786 in Duthill, son of Ludovick Grant, an officer of the Bengal Army, died in Calcutta, India, on 30 August 1818. [BA.2.318]

GRANT, MARGARET, was drummed out of Elgin on 4 December 1753. [RE.2.341]

GRANT, MUNGO, of Knockando, a sasine, 14 December 1713. [NRS.RS28.104.376]

GRANT, PETER, in Alva, 1748. [NRS.E326.1.17]

GRANT, PETER, and ALEXANDER, a tack of lands in Duthel, 1779. [NRS.GD248.533.3/55]

GRANT, ROBERT, of Kincorth, born 3 March 1752, son of David Grant and his wife Margaret, an original member of the North West Company of Canada, died in Kincorth on 10 August 1801. [Cromdale gravestone]

GRANT, THOMAS, of Achoynyany, son of Walter Grant of Arndilly, a sasine, 1722. Banff. [NRS.RS3.119.37]

GRANT, THOMAS, of Auchoyanie, Boharm, 1757. [NRS.E326.1.17]

GRANT, THOMAS, a farmer, was admitted as a burgess of Elgin in 1789. [EBR]

GRANT, Colonel WILLIAM, of Ballindalloch, a sasine, Banff, 1722. [NRS.RS3.120.26]

GRANT, WILLIAM, from Tomnavoulin, Glenlivet, a Jacobite in 1745. [JNE.25]

GRANT, WILLIAM ROY, from Balnacoull, Craigellachie, a Jacobite in 1745. [JNE.2.25]

GRAY, ALEXANDER, a wheelwright, was admitted as a burgess of Elgin in 1751. [EBR]

GRAY, WILLIAM, a tailor in the College of Elgin, 29 September 1702. [RE.2.326]

GREENLAW, JOHN, a weaver, was admitted as a burgess of Elgin in 1748. [EBR]

GREGOR, ROBERT, a shoemaker, was admitted as a burgess of Elgin in 1760. [EBR]

GREIG, ALEXANDER, master of the William of Portsoy trading with Bergen, Norway, in 1750. [NRS.E504.1.3]

GREIG, ......, was admitted as a burgess of Elgin in 1772. [EBR]

GUBBINGS, .........., was admitted as a burgess of Elgin in 1771. [EBR]

GRIGGOR, DUNCAN, a 'charmer' in Elgin in 1734. [RE.2.335]

GUTHRIE, ANNA, spouse of William Hunter minister in Banff, sasines, 21 July 1713 and 31 December 1718. [NRS.RS16.104.2; RS16.113.305]

GUTHRIE, GEORGE, a merchant from Elgin, was admitted as a citizen of Cracow, Poland, in 1624. [SIP.47]

GUTHRIE, GEORGE, a merchant tailor in Cullen, testament, 7 September 1759, Comm. Aberdeen. [NRS]

GUTHRIE, JOHN, Bishop of Moray, was admitted as a burgess of Dundee on 4 July 1633. [EB.146]

HACKETT, JAMES, master of the Sarah of Gamry trading with Bo'ness in 1752. [NRS.E504.1.4]

HADDEN, ALEXANDER, was admitted as a burgess of Elgin in 1785. [EBR]

HARDIE, JOHN, a servant to Provost Brodie, was admitted as a burgess of Elgin in 1752. [EBR]

# THE PEOPLE OF MORAY, BANFF, AND NAIRN, 1700-1799

HARLEY, General, was admitted as a burgess of Elgin on 2 September 1731. [EBR]

HARLEY, JOHN, a gardener, was admitted as a burgess of Elgin in 1707. [EBR]

HARROWAY, GEORGE, a shipmaster in Banff, testament, 4 October 1774, Comm. Aberdeen. [NRS]

HAY, ALEXANDER, clerk to the lieutenancy of the county of Nairn, 1800. [NRS.E328.21

HAY, ANDREW, in Alva, 1748. [NRS.E326.1.17]

HAY, CHARLES, in Rathven, 1748. [NRS.E326.1.17]

HAY, CHARLES, a shoemaker, was admitted as a burgess of Elgin in 1784. [EBR]

HAY, CHARLES, an advocate, was admitted as a burgess of Elgin in 1785. [EBR]

HAY, GEORGE, a merchant in Buckie, a sasine, 28 August 1716. [NRS.RS28.109.298]

HAY, GEORGE, a skipper from Portsoy, an assessor of the Scots Court in Veere, Zealand, in 1739. [NRS.RH11.2]; master of the James and Ann of Portsoy trading between Inverness and Drontheim, Norway, in 1744. [NRS.E504.17.1]

HAY, Dr GEORGE, in Keith, 1757. [NRS.E326.1.17]

HAY, HENRY, was admitted as a burgess of Elgin in 1782. [EBR]

HAY, JAMES, a skipper from Portsoy, an assessor of the Scots Court in Veere, Zealand, in 1737. [NRS.RH11.2]

HAY, JAMES, second son of John Hay a merchant, was admitted as a burgess of Elgin in 1750. [EBR]

HAY, JAMES, a weaver, was admitted as a burgess of Elgin in 1789. [EBR]

HAY, JEAN, widow of John Lorimer a writer in Cullen, testament, 17 December 1754, Comm. Aberdeen. [NRS]

HAY, JOHN, a weaver in Elgin, in 1699. [RE.2.324]

HAY, JOHN, a merchant in Elgin, 1796. [NRS.CS96.1206]

HAY, PATRICK, a Major on Honourable East India Company Service, a sasine, 1794. [NRS.RS.Elgin and Forres. 368]

HAY, ROBERT, was admitted as a burgess of Elgin in 1782. [EBR]

HAY, WILLIAM, master of the Elspet of Cullen trading with Kirkcaldy, Fife, in 1747. [NRS.E504.1.2]; master of the William of Portsoy trading with Newcastle, England, in 1749. [NRS.E504.1.3]

HEINSON, JOHN, from Banff, was admitted as a citizen of Rotterdam, Zealand, on 18 October 1745. [Rotterdam Archives]

HENDERSON, ALEXANDER, a merchant in St Kitts, was admitted as a burgess of Banff in 1770. [BBR]

HENDRY, ALEXANDER, a maltster, was admitted as a burgess of Elgin in 1748. [EBR]

HEPBURN, ROBERT, of Keith, a sasine, 16 July 1701. [NRS.RS16.79.263]

HOSACK, ALEXANDER, born 1728 in Elgin, son of Alexander Hosack and his wife Margaret Cook, a soldier in the French and Indian Wars, settled in New York as a merchant, died in Hackensack, New York, on 9 January 1826. [ANY.I.206]

HOWIE, JAMES, the elder, a merchant in Cullen, a sasine, 27 November 1707. [NRS.RS16.93.318]

HOWISON, JAMES, son of David Howison a gunsmith and Deacon of the Hammermen, was admitted as a burgess of Elgin in 1757. [EBR]

HOYES, ALEXANDER, son of Reverend John Hoyes, [1744-1834], and his wife Janet Reid in Kinloss, a merchant in the West Indies. [F.6.425]

THE PEOPLE OF MORAY, BANFF, AND NAIRN, 1700-1799

HOYES, JOHN, a tack of Knockomie, Forres, 5 November 1762. [NRS.GD347.54]

HOYES, JOHN, minister of Alves from 1777 to 1778. [F.6.376]

HOYES, JOHN, a merchant in Forres, papers, 1793-1809. [NRS.GD248.463.5]

HOYES, JOHN, son of Reverend John Hoyes, [1744-1834], and his wife Janet Reid in Kinloss, a merchant in the West Indies. [F.6.425]

HOYES, WILLIAM, a baillie and merchant in Forres, husband of Margaret Loggan, a deed, 3 October 1798. [NRS.GD347.142]

HUDSON, JOHN, born in Elgin, married Mayken Adrians, born in Arnemuiden, the Netherlands, there on 13 April 1630. [Arnemuiden Marriage Register]

HUMPHREY, JAMES, a goldsmith, was admitted as a burgess of Elgin in 1753. [EBR]

HUNTER, WILLIAM, born 1662, son of Robert Hunter the Provost of Ayr, minister in Banff, sasines 21 July 1713 and 31 December 1718, [NRS.RS16.104.2; S16.113.305]; died 1730, testament, 13 November 1730, Comm. Aberdeen. [NRS][JNE.24]

HUTCHEON, JAMES, second son of James Hutcheon the Deacon of the Weavers, was admitted as a burgess of Elgin in 1751. [EBR]

IMLACH, THOMAS, a packman in Forres, 1758. [NRS.CS228.B4.28]

INNES, ALEXANDER, chief carpenter at HM Dockyard, Port Royal, Jamaica, a sasine, 31 August 1784. [NRS.RS.Elgin and Forres.99]

INNES, ALEXANDER, a tailor, was admitted as a burgess of Elgin in 1776. [EBR]

INNES, DAVID, a square wright in the College of Elgin, sasines, 31 May 1716 and 3 July 1716. [NRS.RS28.109.105; RS28.109.181]

INNES, GEORGE, of Dunkinty, Provost of Elgin, from 1711 to 1714, [RE.2.477], a Jacobite in 1715, [RE.2.379], a sasine, Elgin and Forres, 1731. [NRS.RS3.121.48]

INNES, GEORGE, in Elgin, a letter to William Harper, 29 May 1759. [NRS.CH12.12.810]

INNES, Sir HARRY, the younger of that Ilk, a charter in favour of John Innes of Leuchars, subscribed in Elgin on 25 January 1709. [SRS.Barony of Leuchars Writs.224/19]

INNES, Sir HARRY, versus Emilia Stuart relict of Farquhar McGillivray, a Decreet of Adjudication, 17 February 1726. [SRS.Barony of Innes Writs.159/61]

INNES, JAMES, MD, Provost of Elgin, from 1720 to 1723, 1726 to 1729, 1731 to 1734, 1737 to 1740. [RE.2.477]

INNES, JAMES, minister at Banff, testament, 15 April 1754, Comm. Aberdeen. [NRS]

INNES, JOHN, son of James Innes a merchant in Elgin, a sasine, 3 July 1716. [NRS.RS28.109.181]

INNES, JOHN, of Knockorth, a sasine, Banff, 1724. [NRS.RS3.122.413]

INNES, JOHN, a flax-dresser, late in Cullen now in Elgin, was admitted as a burgess of Elgin in 1760. [EBR]

INNES, JOHN, of Muirfold, residing in Banff, testament, 7 March 1781, Comm. Aberdeen. [NRS]

INNES, PATRICK, a minister in Banff, a sasine, 16 June 1704. [NRS.RS16.85.77]

INNES, ROBERT, MD, Provost of Elgin, from 1717 to 1720, 1723 to 1726. [RE.2.477]

INNES, ROBERT, born 14 September 1745, son of Robert Innes, town clerk of Banff, and his wife Margaret Gilchrist, a merchant in

Gothenburg by 1765, was admitted as a burgess of Montrose in 1791, and a burgess of Newcastle in 1795. [MBR][Northern Scotland.7.146]

INNES, ROBERT, town clerk of Banff, testament, 4 July 1783, Comm. Aberdeen. [NRS]

INNES, THOMAS, from Banff, a member of the Scots Charitable Society of Boston, Massachusetts, in 1748. [NEHGS.SCS]

INNES, WILLIAM, a cooper, was admitted as a burgess of Elgin in 1717. [EBR]

INNES, WILLIAM, a merchant in Elgin, was admitted as a burgess of Elgin in 1763. [EBR]

IZATT, JAMES, master of the Happy Return of Banff trading with Alloa in 1752. [NRS.E504.1.4]

JACK, JAMES, a merchant, was admitted as a burgess of Elgin in 1767. [EBR]

JACK, WILLIAM, a farmer at the Miln of Pluscarden, was admitted as a burgess of Elgin in 1770. [EBR]

JAMIESON, ALEXANDER, son of John Jamieson a baillie, was admitted as a burgess of Elgin in 1775. [EBR]

JAMIESON, JAMES, son of John Jamieson a baillie, was admitted as a burgess of Elgin in 1775. [EBR]

JAMIESON, THOMAS, from Moray, a citizen of Bergen, Norway, in 1632. [SAB]

JEANS, WILLIAM, a wheelwright, was admitted as a burgess of Elgin in 1775. [EBR]

JOHNSTON, ALEXANDER, a brazier, was admitted as a burgess of Elgin in 1711. [EBR]

JOHNSTON, ALEXANDER, a manufacturer, was admitted as a burgess of Elgin in 1796. [EBR]

JOHNSTON, WALTER, master of the Providence of Portsoy trading between Aberdeen and Sunderland, England, in 1743. [NRS.E504.1.1]; trading between Sunderland and Inverness in 1746 [NRS.E504.17.1].

JOHNSTON, WILLIAM, a merchant in Banff, was admitted as a burgess of Elgin in 1778. [EBR]

JUNIS, JOHN, of Muiryfauld, in Grange, 1757. [NRS.E326.1.17]

JUNKEN, GEORGE, former servant to Lord Duffus, was admitted as a burgess of Elgin in 1704. [EBR]

KAY, JOHN, in Easter Alves, eldest son of Andrew Kay a litster burgess of Elgin, a marriage contract with Katherine Leslie, daughter of John Leslie of Middleton, 5 March 1668. [NRS.CS228D.1.5.2]

KAY, WILLIAM, a weaver, was admitted as a burgess of Elgin in 1769. [EBR]

KEITH, ALEXANDER, master of the Caesar of Banff trading between Aberdeen and London in 1744. [NRS.E504.1.1]; master of the Pretty Peggy of Banff trading with Lisbon, Portugal, in 1751. [NRS.E504.1.4]

KEITH, JAMES, formerly in Charleston, South Carolina, died in Blairshinnock, Banffshire, on 14 August 1788. [AJ.2119], Probate, 1810, PCC. [TNA]

KEITH, WILLIAM, son of William Keith, a surgeon in South Carolina, was admitted as a burgess of Banff in 1764. [BBR]

KELLY, ISOBELL, servant to Alexander Kinnaird, was rebuked for winnowing barley on the Sabbath, in 1736. [RE.2.336]

KERR, ....., minister in Rathven, 1748. [NRS.E326.1.17]

KING, ALEXANDER, second son of William King of New Milne, was admitted as a burgess of Elgin in 1749. [EBR]

KING, JAMES, a shoemaker, was admitted as a burgess of Elgin in 1769. [EBR]

KING, RALPH, a schoolmaster in Forres, 3 September 1791. [NRS.GD51.6.908.1-5]

KING, WILLIAM, of Newmill, Provost of Elgin, from 1690 to 1700, 1708 to 1711. [RE.2.476]

KNOX, ......, was admitted as a burgess of Elgin in 1786. [EBR]

KYNOCH, JOHN, a merchant in Aberdeen, was admitted as a burgess of Elgin in 1754. [EBR]

LAING, JOHN, a chapman in Earnside, was admitted as a burgess of Elgin in 1751. [EBR]

LAING, JOHN, an apprentice square-wright, was admitted as a burgess of Elgin in 1757. [EBR]

LAING, JOHN, a skipper in Macduff, inventory, 1822, Comm. Aberdeen. [NRS]

LAING, JOHN, in London, was admitted as a burgess of Elgin in 1777. [EBR]

LATTO, JAMES, master of the James of Banff trading between Trontheim, Norway, and Aberdeen in 1744. [NRS.E504.1.1]

LAURENCE, ....., in Jamaica, was admitted as a burgess of Banff in 1770. [BBR]

LAURIE, JOHN, a mason, was admitted as a burgess of Elgin in 1709. [EBR]

LAWLY, JAMES, in Fordyce, 1753. [NRS.E326.1.17]

LAWSON, JAMES, a merchant in Banff, testaments, 2 February 1749, 21 March 1751, 17 March 1756, and 19 September 1760, Comm. Aberdeen. [NRS]

LEGG, WILLIAM, in Achmore, was appointed the Constable of Fordyce on 31 May 1738. [RB.408]

LEICESTER, ......, an Excise officer, was admitted as a burgess of Elgin in 1709. [EBR]

LESLIE, ALEXANDER, of Kinnivie, the younger, a sasine, Banff, 1703. [NRS.RS3.83.166]

LESLIE, ALEXANDER, a wigmaker, was admitted as a burgess of Elgin in 1705. [EBR]

LESLIE, ALEXANDER, a chapman in Hemprigs, was admitted as a burgess of Elgin in 1770. [EBR]

LESLIE, BESSIE, relict of William Robertson the younger, a burgess of Elgin, a sasine, 1703. [NRS.RS3.83.64]

LESLIE, CHARLES, son of John Leslie of Parkbog, a sasine, Banff, 1702. [NRS.RS3.81.159]

LESLIE, GEORGE, son of William Leslie of Burdsbank, a sasine, Banff, 1706. [NRS.RS3.90.81]

LESLIE, HELEN, daughter of William Leslie of Burdsbank, and spouse of William Stevenson minister at Fordyce, a sasine 1 October 1706. [NRS.RS16.90.81]

LESLIE, JAMES, a writer in Edinburgh, was admitted as a burgess of Elgin in 1752. [EBR]

LESLIE, JAMES, a wright, was admitted as a burgess of Elgin in 1766. [EBR]

LESLIE, JAMES, possibly from Elgin, died in Jamaica around 1783. [Elgin Town Council minutes, 15.11.1783]

LESLIE, JAMES, born 31 May 1797 in Elgin, son of Reverend William William Leslie and his wife Margaret Sinclair, died in Bermuda on 4 July 1819. [F.3.397]

LESLIE, JANET, daughter of Patrick Leslie a tailor in Elgin, versus Betty Mackenzie, spouse of Major Gordon Graham of the Royal Regiment of Highlanders, a Process of Scandal, 1750. [NRS.CC8.6.331]

LESLIE, JOHN, baptised 13 October 1749 in Rothes, son of Alexander Leslie of Balnageith and his wife Anna Duff, a merchant in St Augustine, East Florida, in 1786. [IT.21][Florida Historical Review.18.1]

LESLIE, LACHLAN, chamberlain to the Earl of Leven, a sasine, Banff, 1705. [NRS.RS3.87.375]

LESLIE, PATRICK, the sheriff clerk of Banff, a sasine, 1714. [NRS.RS3.104.420]

LESLIE, ROBERT, of Edintore, a sasine, Banff, 1705. [NRS.RS3.87.298]

LESLIE, ROBERT, master of the Jean and Mary of Banff trading with Bilbao, Spain, in 1750. [NRS.E504.1.3]; master of the Vernon of Banff trading with Norway, Newcastle, and Cadiz, Spain, in 1749-1751. [NRS.E504.1.3]; master of the Jean and Mary of Banff trading with Bilbao, Newcastle, Alloa, Flekkefjord, Danzig, and Venice in 1751-1752. [NRS.E504.1.4]

LESLIE, ROBERT, baptised 3 February 1758 in Rothes, son of Alexander Leslie of Balnageith and his wife Anna Duff, a merchant in St Augustine, East Florida, in 1786. [IT.19]

LESLIE, WILLIAM, of Belnageith, Forres, a contract, 7 March 1723. [NRS.GD36.33]

LESLIE, WILLIAM, master of the Vernon of Banff trading with Kristiansand, Newcastle, Bumblefjord, and Rotterdam from 1751 to 1753. [NRS.E504.1.4]

LESLIE, WILLIAM, born 2 July 1794, son of Reverend William Leslie and his wife Margaret Sinclair in Llanbryd, a surgeon on Honourable East India Company Service, died in India on 10 June 1831. [F.6.397]

LESLIE, WILLIAM, born 26 December 1798 in Duffus, a member of the firm of Gibson and Company, tailors, died 11 June 1841. [Scotch Burial Ground gravestone, Calcutta, India.]

LIVIE, ALEXANDER, a baker. was admitted as a burgess of Elgin in 1755. [EBR]

LOCKHART, GRACE, daughter of George Lockhart of Carnwath, relict of the Earl of Aboyne, spouse to James Stewart, Earl of Moray, a sasine, 1735. [NRS.RS3.148.57]

LOGGAN, ANN, wife of Alexander Forsyth a merchant in Forres, heir to her grandfather baillie Robert Loggan a dyer there, September 1762. [NRS.S/H]

LOGGAN, JEAN, heir to her father Robert Loggan a dyer and baillie of Forres, 18 August 1762. [NRS.SH]

LOGGAN, MARGARET, daughter of Robert Loggan minister at Rafford, heir to her grandfather baillie Robert Loggan a dyer in Forres, September 1762. [NRS.S/H]

LOGIE, GEORGE, son of Andrew Logie of Loanhead, a sasine, 1706, Banff. [NRS.RS3.90.81]

LOGIE, Major WILLIAM, son of Alexander Logie, [1756-1836], and his wife Agnes Cluny, [1757-1823], settled in America. [Speymouth Essil gravestone]

LOGIE, WILLIAM, born 10 August 1781, son of James Logie and his wife Elizabeth Gordon in Boat of Bog, Speymouth, an officer of the Bengal Army, died in Saugor, Bengal, India, on 13 January 1828. [BA.3.74]

LONGMUIR, JAMES, in Portsoy, was appointed the Constable of Fordyce on 7 April 1741. [RB.409]

LORIMER, JOHN, a merchant in Portsoy, testaments, 20 November 1770 and 8 December 1772, Comm. Aberdeen. [NRS]

LORIMER, PATRICK, in Fordyce, 1753. [NRS.E326.1.17]

LORIMER, PATRICK, in Portsoy, testament, 15 February 1771, Comm. Aberdeen. [NRS]

LOWSON, HARRY, a gardener in Banff, father of James and Patrick, testament, 3 September 1729, Comm. Aberdeen. [NRS]

LUPTON, ……, an Excise officer, was admitted as a burgess of Elgin in 1709. [EBR]

MCBAIN, KENNETH, was admitted as a burgess of Elgin in 1782. [EBR]

MCBEAN, ARCHIBALD, born 1709, a farmer in Aberlour, with wife Catherine Cameron born 1714, and son Alexander, emigrated from Inverness to Georgia aboard the *Prince of Wales* on 20 October 1735, dead by 1740. [ESG.83]

MCBEAN, WILLIAM, born 1758 in Inverness-shire, graduated MA from King's College, Aberdeen, in 1778, minister at Little Kirk, Elgin, in 1787, then at Moy and Dalrossie from 1788 to 1792, finally at Alves from 1792 until his death on 5 April 1818. Husband of [1] Elizabeth Duff, parents of Alexander and Isabella, [2] Janet Leslie. [F.6.377]

MCBEATH, ……., from America, was admitted as a burgess of Elgin in 1787. [EBR]

MCCULL, THOMAS, was admitted as a burgess of Elgin in 1786. [EBR]

MCCULLOCH, DAVID, a merchant in Forres, 1773. [NRS.CS236.M3.19]

MCCULLOCH, THOMAS, minister at Birnie from 1708 until 1709. [F.6.379]

MCDONALD, FRANCIS, born 1795, died at Morant Bay, Jamaica, on 19 June 1833. [Inveraven gravestone]

MCDONALD, JAMES, born 1794, late of Morant Bay, Jamaica, died in Charleston of Aberlour on 6 April 1836. [Inveraven gravestone]

MCDONALD, MARY, widow of Dougal McQueen, and their son Lachlan McQueen, a tack of Achtatipper, Duthil, in 1779. [NRS.GD248.533.3/65]

MCDONALD, WILLIAM, a smith, was admitted as a burgess of Elgin in 1767. [EBR]

MCDUELL, THOMAS, an Excise officer in Banff, testament, 20 June 1729, Comm. Aberdeen. [NRS]

MCGILLAWREA, JOHN, a butcher in Elgin, was admitted as a burgess of Elgin in 1752. [EBR]

MCGILLIGAN, GEORGE, master of the Unity of Banff trading with Bergen, Norway, in 1750. [NRS.E504.1.3]; master of the Unity Jean of Whitehills trading with Alloa and with Norway in 1750, Bo'ness and Kristiansand, Norway, in 1752. [NRS.E504.1.3/4]; master of the Unity Jean of Banff trading with Lisbon, Portugal, and Bergen, Norway, in 1752. [NRS.E504.1.4]

MCGILLIGAN, GEORGE, born 1728, late Provost of Banff, died there on 30 January 1798. [SM.XL.214]

MCGOWEN, ....., was admitted as a burgess of Elgin in 1695. [EBR]

MCGREGOR, CHARLES, son of Grigor McGregor, [1770-1854], and his wife Ann, [1787-1838], settled in Trinidad. [Cromdale gravestone]

MCGREGOR, DUNCAN, a reputed charmer in Elgin, 12 December 1734. [RE.2.379]

MCGREGOR, GRIGOR, son of Colquhoun MacGregor [died 1847], and Margaret Leslie [died 1810], a merchant in Mauritius. [Cromdale gravestone]

MCGREGOR, ROBERT, a merchant in Forres, 3 October 1796. [NRS.GD248.533.5/58]

MCHENRY, JAMES, born in Forres in1788, a merchant in Savanna, Georgia, died on 22 September 1826 in Lexington, Oglethorpe County, Georgia. ['Georgia Republican', 10.10.1826]

MCINTOSH, AGNES, was banished from Elgin for fornication with David Fairer a chapman, in 1707. [RE.2.327]

MCINTOSH, CHARLES, a physician in Jamaica, was admitted as a burgess of Banff in 1770. [BBR]

MCINTOSH, DONALD, a shipmaster in Inverness, was admitted as a burgess of Elgin in 1760. [EBR]

MCINTOSH, DUNCAN, born 1779, son of Andrew MacIntosh, a merchant in Forres, a surgeon, died in Spain on 10 May 1813. [SM.75.478]

MACINTOSH, JAMES, a hirer in Forres, 1760. [NRS.CS228.A3.13]

MCINTOSH, JAMES, born 1754 in Strathdearn, son of William Roy McIntosh of Dell and his wife Marjory, emigrated to New York in 1776, a merchant there, died on 4 November 1811. [ANY.I.176]

MCINTOSH, JOHN, a skipper in Banff, inventory, 1818, Comm. Aberdeen. [NRS]

MCINTOSH, THOMAS, a tack of Eil, Duthil,1780. [NRS.GD248.533.5/27]

MCINTOSH, Colonel, was admitted as a burgess of Elgin in 1784. [EBR]

MCKANCY, ALEXANDER, master of the brigantine Expedition of Portsoy bound from Banff to Kristiansand, Norway, in May 1807. [NRS.E504.5.1]

MCKAY, Major AENEAS, was admitted as a burgess of Elgin in 1689. [EBR]

MACKAY, JAMES, a merchant in Forres, 1790 [NRS.CS228.MC6.27.2]

MCKAY, JOHN, master of the sloop Active of Banff bound from Banff to Kristiansand, Norway, in April 1807. [NRS.E504.5.1]

MCKEAN, JAMES, a chapman, was admitted as a burgess of Elgin in 1730. [EBR]; late merchant in Elgin, a mortification for the poor of Elgin, 1738. [RE.2.337]

MCKEAN, JOHN, born 1652 in Elgin, son of John McKean, graduated MA from King's College, Aberdeen, in 1668, a schoolmaster in Cromarty, later in Elgin, minister of Birnie from 1696 until 1703. [F.6.379]

MCKEAN, ...., a baillie, was admitted as a burgess of Elgin in 1695. [EBR]

MCKENZIE, ALEXANDER, a weaver in the College of Elgin, was admitted as a burgess of Elgin in 1748. [EBR]

MCKENZIE, ALEXANDER, a weaver, son of Alexander McKenzie a weaver, was admitted as a burgess of Elgin in 1760. [EBR]

MCKENZIE, ANN, spouse to John Dunbar of Burgie an advocate, a sasine, 1723, Elgin and Forres. [NRS.RS3.121.289]

MCKENZIE, CHARLES, a merchant, son of Kenneth McKenzie the elder, an apothecary, was admitted as a burgess of Elgin in 1760. [EBR]

MCKENZIE, HECTOR, a former soldier of the British Fusiliers, a prisoner in Banff Tolbooth, accused of theft and hamesucken, of David Christie in Auchmilly, in May 1719. [RB.397]

MCKENZIE, JAMES, a farmer, was admitted as a burgess of Elgin in 1771. [EBR]

MCKENZIE, KENNETH, a bailiff of Elgin, a Jacobite in 1715. [RE.2.379]

MACKIE, JAMES, in Fordyce, 1753. [NRS.E326.1.17]

MACKIE, JAMES, a merchant in Portsoy, testaments, 1756/1757, [Comm. Aberdeen. NRS]

MACKIE, GEORGE, a merchant in Portsoy, testaments, 1756/1757. [Comm. Aberdeen. NRS]

MACKIE, JAMES, a merchant in Portsoy, testament, 18 November 1755, Comm. Aberdeen. [NRS]

MACKIE, JAMES, in St Vincent, was admitted as a burgess of Banff in 1778. [BBR]

MACKIE, THOMAS, in Quebec, son of James Mackie a merchant in Findhorn, a sasine, 1801. [NRS.RS.Elgin and Forres.567]

MACKIE, WILLIAM, in Jamaica, later in Forres, testament, 1820. [NRS.CC16.5.3.189]

MCKILLANDREA, BENJAMIN, and his spouse Margaret Clerk, daughter of Alexander Clerk in the College of Elgin, a sasine, Elgin and Forres, 1716. [NRS.RS3.109.105]

MCKINNON, ALEXANDER, a merchant in Leghorn, Italy, was admitted as a burgess of Banff in 1786. [BBR]

MCLACHLAN, WILLIAM, a barber in Cullen, testament, 21 July 1743, Comm. Aberdeen. [NRS]

MCLEAN, LACHLAN, a merchant in Danzig, was admitted as a burgess of Banff in 1786. [BBR]

MCLEOD, ALEXANDER, born 1792, son of Captain William McLeod [1761-1833]. A Lieutenant Colonel of the 61$^{st}$ Regiment, died in India on 18 August 1849. [Bellie gravestone]

MCPHERSON, DUNCAN, a merchant in Banff, testament, 9 January 1759, Comm. Aberdeen. [NRS]

MCPHERSON, JOHN, from Strathspey, a member of the Scots Charitable Society of Boston, Massachusetts, in 1758. [NEHGS/SCS]

THE PEOPLE OF MORAY, BANFF, AND NAIRN, 1700-1799

MCPHERSON, KENNETH, in Nairn, a deed, 2 July 1769. [NRS.RD.4.209/1.790]

MACPHERSON, ROBERT, born 1711, a farmer in Alvie, emigrated via Inverness aboard the Prince of Wales bound for Georgia on 20 October 1735. [ESG.87]

MCQUEEN, DOUGAL, of Polochaig, Findhorn, 25 September 1799. [NRS.GD176.884]

MADDEN, SAMUEL, a Captain of the 15$^{th}$ Regiment of Foot, married Margaret Cumming, daughter of Colonel Cumming of Altyre, in Elgin on 8 October 1798. [SM.XL.729]

MAITLAND, CHARLES, a Major in Honourable East India Company Service, a sasine, 15 May 1794. [NRS.RS.Elgin and Forres.367]

MALCOLM, JOHN, a maltman, was admitted as a burgess of Elgin in 1757. [EBR]

MANN, JAMES, born 15 December 1795 in Elgin, son of John Mann and his wife Janet Laing, a husbandman who emigrated to Manchester, Massachusetts, settled in New Chester, New Hampshire, in 1812, moved to Danby, N.H., in October 1820, later in Hampstead, N.H., in November 1820, naturalised in Rockingham, N.H., on 11 March 1833.

MANTACH, Reverend ROBERT, born 1792, son of John Mantach, a farmer in Dundurcas, and his wife Jane, died 18 December 1854 on Boaz Island, Bermuda. [Rothes Dundurcas gravestone]

MARK, FRANCIS, son of James Mark a merchant in Banff, testament, 13 December 1749, Comm. Aberdeen. [NRS]

MARK, JAMES, a merchant in Banff, testaments, 1732/1751, Comm. Aberdeen. [NRS]

MARK, JOHN, a merchant and late Provost of Banff, testament, 13 July 1732, Comm. Aberdeen. [NRS]

MARSHALL, GEORGE, son of William Marshall and his wife Jean Giles, a Lieutenant of the 62$^{nd}$ Regiment, died in Spain in 1812. [Bellie gravestone]

MARSHALL, JAMES, jr., a gardener, was admitted as a burgess of Elgin in 1770. [EBR]

MARSHALL, JOHN, son of William Marshall and his wife Jean Giles, an Army Captain, died in Madras, India, in 1829. [Bellie gravestone]

MASON, ALEXANDER, a weaver, was admitted as a burgess of Elgin in 1775. [EBR]

MASSON, JOHN, in Tain, was admitted as a burgess of Elgin in 1689. [EBR]

MASSON, ROBERT, a servant to Provost James Robertson, was admitted as a burgess of Elgin in 1758. [EBR]

MASSON, WILLIAM, master of the Peggie of Banff trading with Bo'ness in 1752. [NRS.E504.1.4]

MATHEW, ALEXANDER, a cooper, was admitted as a burgess of Elgin in 1754. [EBR]

MATHEW, WILLIAM, clerk to Provost George Brown, was admitted as a burgess of Elgin in1785. [EBR]

MATHEW, ....., an apothecary in Aberdeen, was admitted as a burgess of Elgin in 1686. [EBR]

MAULE, JAMES, in Darnaway, a letter, 23 October 1781. [NRS.GD1.640.23]

MAY, PETER, factor to the Earl of Findlator, was admitted as a burgess of Elgin in 1772. [EBR]

MELLIS, ARCHIBALD, a mason, was admitted as a burgess of Elgin in 1774. [EBR]

MELLICE, JAMES, a merchant, was admitted as a burgess of Elgin in 1763. [EBR]

MENZIES, ANNE, daughter of Colin Menzies a merchant in Elgin, testament, 20 September 1759, Comm. Aberdeen. [NRS]

MILL, JOHN, son of Andrew Mill and his wife Janet Ligertwood in Meikle Creich, Banffshire, a traveller in Poland in 1601. [MSC.II.58]

MILL, WILLIAM, son of Andrew Mill and his wife Margaret in Newton of Troine, Abercharder, Banffshire, settled in Neustadtyn, Pomerania, by 1595. [MSC.II.31]

MILLER, ALEXANDER, a merchant in Banff, testament, 16 July 1765, Comm. Aberdeen. [NRS]

MILLER, JOHN, was admitted as a burgess of Elgin in 1782. [EBR]

MILNE, ALEXANDER, at the Mill of Alva, was appointed the Constable of Alva on 31 May 1738, and again on 7 April 1741. [RB.408-409]

MILNE, GEORGE, in Paddocklaw, was appointed the Constable of Banff on 7 April 1741. [RB.409]

MILNE, JOHN, a skipper in Banff, testament, 23 January 1740, Comm. Aberdeen. [NRS]

MILNE, JOHN, in Monblaiton, was appointed constable in Gamrie on 7 April 1741. [RB.409]

MILNE, MOSES, son of James Milne, a merchant in Bergen, Norway, was admitted as a burgess of Banff in 1769. [BBR]

MILNE, THOMAS, a merchant in Batavia, Dutch East Indies, son of James Milne of Milnefield, Elgin, a sasine, 1830. [NRS.RS.Elgin and Forres.371]

MILNE, WILLIAM, son of James Milne, a merchant in Bergen, Norway, was admitted as a burgess of Banff in 1764. [BBR]

MILNE, ......, son of the Provost of Montrose, was admitted as a burgess of Elgin in 1706. [EBR]

MIRELAND, ......, was admitted as a burgess of Elgin in 1709. [EBR]

MISSEN, Major, was admitted as a burgess of Elgin in 1778. [EBR]

MITCHELL, ALEXANDER, a weaver, was admitted as a burgess of Elgin in 1769. [EBR]

MITCHELL, DONALD, MA, born 6 January 1792, son of Reverend Donald Mitchell and his wife Christian Gordon in Ardlach, a missionary in India, died 20 November 1823. [F.6.432]

MITCHELL, JOHN, a malt-man, was admitted as a burgess of Elgin in 1755. [EBR]

MITCHELL, JOHN, an inn-keeper, was admitted as a burgess of Elgin in 1763. [EBR]

MITCHELL, JOHN, born 22 November 1793, son of Reverend Donald Mitchell and his wife Christian Gordon in Ardlach, a missionary in Ceylon. [F.6.432]

MITCHELL, ROBERT, was admitted as a burgess of Elgin in 1782. [EBR]

MITCHELL, WILLIAM, a weaver, was admitted as a burgess of Elgin in 1770. [EBR]

MITCHELL, WILLIAM, in Elgin, a letter, 11 April 1778. [NRS.CH12.24.274]

MITCHELSON, DAVID, late of New York, a sasine, 1800. [NRS.RS.Elgin and Forres.549]

MONRO, ALEXANDER, from Inverness, was appointed music master, precentor, and session clerk of Elgin in 1709. [RE.2.410]

# THE PEOPLE OF MORAY, BANFF, AND NAIRN, 1700-1799

MOORE, JOHN, from Forres, and his wife Betty Taylor, settled in Moresville, Delaware County, New York, in 1772. [NYGBR.25]

MORICE, DAVID, a chapman, was admitted as a burgess of Elgin in 1761. [EBR]

MORICE, DAVID, in Aberdeen, was admitted as a burgess of Elgin in1785. [EBR]

MORICE, JAMES, a square-wright, was admitted as a burgess of Elgin in 1751. [EBR]

MORISON, ELSPET, in Banff, testament, 2 March 1793, Comm. Aberdeen. [NRS]

MORRISON, GEORGE, master of the Jean of Banff, trading with Gothenburg, Sweden, in 1806. [NRS.E504.5.1]

MORRISON, JAMES, and Company, merchants in Forres, letters, 1783-1789. [NRS.B59.37.9.19-23]

MORRISON, JOHN, master of a schooner Britannia of Macduff bound from Banff for Christiansand, Norway, in May 1807. [NRS.E504.5.1]

MORISON, WALTER, in Deskford, 1748. [NRS.E326.1.17]

MORTIMER, EDWARD, born 1768, son of Alexander Mortimer, a burgess of Forres, and his wife Mary Smith, a merchant in Pictou, Nova Scotia, died there on 10 October 1819. [Chronicles of Keith, Glasgow, 1880]

MORTIMER, ROBERT, a merchant in Banff, testament, 22 February 1723, Comm. Aberdeen. [NRS]

MOWAT, RODGER, from Elgin, and Helen Wilson from Linlithgow, were married in the Scots Kirk in Rotterdam on 9 March 1712. [Rotterdam Archives]

MUIL, JOHN, a shoemaker, was admitted as a burgess of Elgin in 1751. [EBR]

MUIR, JOHN, a hook-maker in Cullen, testament, 2 July 1762, Comm. Aberdeen. [NRS]

MUNRO, JAMES, was educated at King's College, Aberdeen, from 1729 to 1733, minister of Kinloss from 1752 to 1775, minister of Alves from 1775 to his death on 24 June 1780. Husband of Mary Gordon, parents of George, Margaret and others. [F.6.376]

MUNRO, JOHN, a dyker, was admitted as a burgess of Elgin in 1775. [EBR]

MUNRO, WILLIAM, a merchant in Banff, testament, 16 March 1765, Comm. Aberdeen. [NRS]

MURDOCH, ALEXANDER, in Glasgow, son of Robert Murdoch a merchant in Elgin, was admitted as a burgess of Elgin in 1792. [EBR]

MURDOCH, DAVID, a butcher, was admitted as a burgess of Elgin in 1782. [EBR]

MURDOCH, DUNCAN, a chapman, was admitted as a burgess of Elgin in 1751. [EBR]

MURDOCH, GEORGE, a baker, was admitted as a burgess of Elgin in 1776. [EBR]

MURDOCH, JEAN, rebuked for drying plaiding on the Sabbath in 1764 in Elgin. [RE.2.345]

MURDOCH, JOHN, a postman, was admitted as a burgess of Elgin in 1748. [EBR]

MURDOCH, JOHN, in Inshallan in the Glen of Pluscarden, a mortification in favour of the poor, 1754. [RE.2.342]

MURDOCH, JOHN, a wright, was admitted as a burgess of Elgin in 1766. [EBR]

MURDOCH, ROBERT, a chapman, was admitted as a burgess of Elgin in 1749. [EBR]

MURRAY, ALEXANDER, born 1701, son of Reverend James Murray in Grange, minister of Birnie from 1743 until his death on 13 August 1765. [F.6.379]

MURRAY, ALEXANDER, born in Duffus on 10 June 1757, son of Reverend Alexander Murray and his wife Isabel Gordon, an officer of the Bengal Army, died in Calcutta, India, on 6 December 1796. [BA.3.357]

MURRAY, ANNA, in Cullen, 1748. [NRS.E326.1.17]

MURRAY, GILBERT, a gardener in Banff, heir to his brother Alexander Murray, 18 March 1766. [NRS.S/H]

MURRAY, JAMES, a soldier from Forres, married Anna Holms in the English church in Middelburg, Zealand, on 14 December 1617. [Arnemuiden Marriage Register]

MURRAY, JOHN, sometime in Demerara, lately in Portsoy, testament, 2 July 1795, Comm. Aberdeen. [NRS]

MURRAY, JOHN, born 12 March 1781 in Moray, son of Andrew Murray and his wife Jean Grant, an officer of the Bengal Army, died in Cawnpore, India, on 25 April 1802. [BA.3.361]

MURRAY, JOHN, in Demerara, later in Portsoy, testament, 1795, Comm. Aberdeen. [NRS]

MURRAY, THOMAS, town clerk of Cullen, testament, 4 January 1733, Comm. Aberdeen. [NRS]

MURRAY, WILLIAM, from Banff, a member of the Scots Charitable Society of Boston, Massachusetts, in 1751. [NEHGS/SCS]

MURRAY, WILLIAM, in Latiune, Jamaica, was admitted as a burgess of Banff in 1799. [BBR]

## THE PEOPLE OF MORAY, BANFF, AND NAIRN, 1700-1799

MURTRAE, GEORGE, a merchant in Banff, testaments, 12 August 1784, and 21 February 1785, Comm. Aberdeen. [NRS]

NICOL, ALEXANDER, an indentured servant bound for Georgia who may have absconded, 19 July 1738. [Elgin Kirk Session Register]

NAUGHTIE, ALEXANDER, a tailor, was admitted as a burgess of Elgin in 1760. [EBR]

NAUGHTIE, WILLIAM, a tailor in Bishopsmilne, was admitted as a burgess of Elgin in 1757. [EBR]

NICOL, JAMES, a skipper in Gardenstown, testament, 1805 Comm. Aberdeen. [NRS]

NICOL, JAMES, master of the brigantine Isobella of Banff, bound from Banff to Trontheim, Norway, in March 1807. [NRS.E504.5.1]

NICOL, JOHN, a carpenter in Banff, testament, 5 March 1742, Comm. Aberdeen. [NRS]

NICOLL, JOHN, a merchant in Lossiemouth, was admitted as a burgess of Elgin in 1760. [EBR]

NICOL, PETER, master of the Sarah of Gamry trading with Kirkcaldy, Fife, in 1749. [NRS.E504.1.3]; master of the Sarah of Banff trading with Newcastle, England, in 1750. [NRS.E504.1.3]

NICOLSON, ALEXANDER, a tailor in Forres, a sasine, 7 December 1716. [NRS.RS28.110.151]

NICOLSON, ISOBEL, daughter of Alexander Nicolson a tailor in Forres, a sasine, 7 December 1716. [NRS.RS28.110.151]

NICOLSON, MARGARET, daughter of Alexander Nicolson a tailor in Forres, and spouse of Thomas Boyd a merchant there, a sasine, 7 December 1716. [NRS.RS28.110.151]

NILSON, JOHN, master of the Diana of Banff, bound from Banff to Archangel, Russia, in June 1806. [NRS.E504.5.1]

# THE PEOPLE OF MORAY, BANFF, AND NAIRN, 1700-1799

OGG, JOHN, a merchant in Banff, testaments, 26 June 1760 and 28 October 1760, Comm. Aberdeen. [NRS]

OGILVIE, ALEXANDER, a skipper in Banff, testament, 12 February 1729, Comm. Aberdeen. [NRS]

OGILVIE, ANNA, widow of Alexander Hay late burgess of Cullen, testament, 2 July 1734, Comm. Aberdeen. [NRS]

OGILVIE, CHARLES, from Banffshire, in South Carolina in the 1770s. [NRS.NRAS .0426, box 8, bundles 31-34]

OGILVIE, GEORGE, was admitted as a burgess of Elgin in 1760. [EBR]

OGILVIE, or DUFF, Mrs ISOBEL, in Macduff, testament, 12 June 1798, Comm. Aberdeen. [NRS]

OGILVIE, JAMES, a mason in Elgin, late tacksman of the quarries of Quarrywood, a decree, 1720. [NRS.GD36.31]

OGILVIE, JAMES, bailie of Banff in 1724. [RB.402]

OGILVIE, JAMES, master of the Friendship of Portsoy trading between Aberdeen, Rotterdam, Zealand, and Bergen, Norway, in 1742. [NRS.E504.1.1]

OGILVIE, JAMES, in Rathven, 1748. [NRS.E326.1.17]

OGILVIE, JAMES, born 1747, son of William Ogilvie and his wife Helen Baird, died in Jamaica on 6 June 1774. [Banff gravestone]

OGILVIE, JOHN, son of Andrew Ogilvie the Dean of Guild, was admitted as a burgess of Elgin in 1760. [EBR]

OGILVIE, JOHN, born 1753, son of William Ogilvie and his wife Helen Baird, died in Antigua on 30 August 1770. [Banff gravestone]

OGILVIE, THOMAS, a dyer in Banff, testament, 19 September, Comm. Aberdeen. [NRS]

OGILVIE, Dr WILLIAM, a physician in Banff, testament, 17 August 1737, Comm. Aberdeen. [NRS]

OGILVIE, WILLIAM, born 1742, son of William Ogilvie and his wife Helen Baird, died in 'Bassora' [Basra, Iraq] on 9 May 1783. [Banff gravestone]

OGILVIE, WILLIAM, a merchant in Banff, testament, 14 March 1788, Comm. Aberdeen. [NRS]

OGILVIE, Mistress, in Deskford, 1748. [NRS.E326.1.17]

OLIPHANT, JAMES, of Gask, a sasine, Banff, 1709. [NRS.RS3.96.340]

OLIPHANT, PATRICK, a sasine, 1705. Banff. [NRS.RS3.88.210]

ORD, ALEXANDER, a merchant baillie of Cullen, testament, 16 November 1738, Comm. Aberdeen. [NRS]

ORD, ELSPET, widow of James Abercrombie a bailie of Cullen, testament, 28 April 1782, Comm. Aberdeen. [NRS]

ORD, HELEN, widow of William Baird late bailie of Cullen, testament, 11 March 1726, Comm. Aberdeen. [NRS]

ORD, JAMES, a bailie of Cullen, testament, 4 July 1739, Comm. Aberdeen. [NRS]

ORD, JAMES, master of the Perseverance Packet of Banff bound from Banff for Kristiansand, Norway, in August 1806. [NRS.E504.5.11]

PANTON, ADAM, a merchant in Banff, testaments, 1733/1736, Comm. Aberdeen. [NRS]

PANTON, ……, a factor, was admitted as a burgess of Elgin in 1694. [EBR]

PARIS, JEAN, a vagrant, was drummed out of Elgin and banished from the province of Moray on 24 June 1708. [RE.2.378]

PATERSON, ALEXANDER, master of the Janet of Gamrie trading with Kirkcaldy, Fife, in 1748. [NRS.E504.1.2]

# THE PEOPLE OF MORAY, BANFF, AND NAIRN, 1700-1799

PATERSON, ALEXANDER, master of the Mary of Portsoy trading between Stornaway and Leghorn, Italy, in 1774. [NRS.E504.33.1]

PATERSON, ALEXANDER, a merchant in Banff, testaments, 15 December 1775 and 6 March 1777, Comm. Aberdeen. [NRS]

PATERSON, GEORGE, master of the Speedwell of Banff trading with Kirkcaldy, Fife, in 1747. [NRS.E504.1.2]

PATERSON, ROBERT, was admitted as a burgess of Elgin in 1682. [EBR]

PATERSON, ROBERT, born on 17 July 1782, son of Reverend Robert Paterson and his wife Margaret Collie in Spynie, a surgeon on Honourable East India Company Service, died in Calcutta, India, in December 1829. [F.6.407]

PATERSON, WILLIAM, master of the Nelly of Macduff from Christiansand, Norway, to Banff in August 1806. [NRS.E504.5.1]

PETERKIN, ALEXANDER, a merchant in Forres, and his spouse Margaret Smith, a bond, 4 June 1730. [NRS.GD23.5.229]

PETERKIN, JAMES, a merchant in Forres, a bill of exchange, 17 August 1781. [NRS.GD1.675.12]

PETERKIN, JOHN, master of the Ann of Burghead arrived in Banff from Inverness in June 1806. [NRS.E504.5.1]

PETRIE, ARTHUR, in Nairn, a letter, 19 June 1779. [NRS.CH12.24.3269]

PETRIE, JAMES, in Inchdruer, was appointed the Constable of Banff on 31 May 1738. [RB.408]

PETRIE, JOHN, schoolmaster at Milton Brodie, was admitted as a burgess of Elgin in 1694. [EBR]

PETRIE, JOHN, was appointed schoolmaster at Pluscarden on 8 March 1747. [RE.2.340]

PHILIP, ROBERT, a glover, was admitted as a burgess of Elgin in 1775. [EBR]

PIPER, JOHN, in Oldton of Melross, was appointed constable in Gamrie on 7 April 1741. [RB.409]

PIRIE, GEORGE, was admitted as a burgess of Elgin in 1783. [EBR]

PREIST, ISABELLA, spouse of Robert White, was accused of calling Agnes Falconer, spouse of John Bell a merchant, a witch and causing the death of John Smith, a merchant, and his cow, in Elgin in 1706. [RE.2.327]

PROCTOR, WILLIAM, a chapman, was admitted as a burgess of Elgin in 1749. [EBR]

PROTT, WILLIAM, a sailor in Portsoy, testament, 18 October 1784, Comm. Aberdeen. [NRS]

PURSS, JOHN, born in Elgin on 12 December 1732, son of Alexander Purss, a tailor, and his wife Isabel Blenshel, settled in Canada before 1762, a merchant and a public official, died in Quebec on 8 April 1843. [DCB]

PURSE, WILLIAM, a weaver, was admitted as a burgess of Elgin in 1760. [EBR]

RAFFAN, ALEXANDER, master of the sloop Minerva of Macduff, bound from Banff to Kristiansand, Norway, in April 1807. [NRS.E504.5.1]

RAINIE, ....., was admitted as a burgess of Elgin in 1784. [EBR]

RAIT, DAVID, master of the Deskford of Portsoy trading with Rotterdam, Zealand, in 1750. [NRS.E504.1.3]

RAMSAY, ARCHIBALD, a smith, , was admitted as a burgess of Elgin in 1753. [EBR]

RAMSAY, BATHIA, in Cullen, 1748. [NRS.E326.1.17]

RAMSAY, SAMUEL, a smith, was admitted as a burgess of Elgin in 1768. [EBR]

RAMSAY, WILLIAM, a periwig maker in Elgin in 1701. [RE.2.325]

RAMSAY, WILLIAM, a smith in Bishopmiln, son of Archibald Smith, a smith in Bishopmiln, and grandson of Samuel Ramsay in Duffus, both freemen of Elgin, was admitted as a burgess of Elgin in 1774. [EBR]

REID, BARBARA, 'a naughty person' in the College of Elgin' to be banished, in 1760. [RE.2.343]

REID, JAMES, born 3 January 1777, son of William Reid, town clerk of Banff, and his wife Margaret Innes, a merchant in Gothenburg, Sweden, died there on 17 March 1813. [Northern Scotland.7.1.147]

REID, JOHN, in the Mill of Durn, was appointed the Constable of Fordyce on 7 April 1741. [RB.409]

REID, JOHN, a skipper in Lossie, testament, 1820, Comm. Moray. [NRS]

REID, P., a shoemaker in Pluscarden, was admitted as a burgess of Elgin in 1760. [EBR]

RICHARDS, JAMES, a shoemaker, was admitted as a burgess of Elgin in 1774. [EBR]

RIDDELL, Sir JAMES, was admitted as a burgess of Forres on 29 April 1723. [NRS.GD1.35.28]

RIDIE, JAMES, in St Fergus, Banff, 1757. [NRS.E326.1.17]

RIND, JANET, was banished from Elgin on 25 August 1702. [RE.2.326]

RITCHIE, ALEXANDER, in Fochabers, a contract, 1710. [NRS.CR8.202]

RITCHIE, ANDREW, from Forres, Morayshire, in Konigsberg, Lithuania, was granted a birth brief by Aberdeen Town Council on 15 April 1664. [APB.I]

RITCHIE, JOHN, a merchant, died in Elgin on 7March 1798. [Elgin gravestone]

RITCHIE, WILLIAM, master of the Elizabeth of Portsoy trading between Rotterdam, Zealand, and Inverness in 1742. [NRS.E504.17.1]

ROBERTSON, ALEXANDER, in Jamaica, son of James Robertson of Bishopmills, a sasine, 1768. [NRS.RS.Elgin.8.87]; Naval Officer of Kingston, Jamaica, died at Port Royal Harbour, there, on 19 September 1791. [SM.53.568]

ROBERTSON, ALEXANDER, a merchant in Portsoy, testament, 8 June 1791, Comm. Aberdeen. [NRS]

ROBERTSON, CHRISTIAN, rebuked for gathering lint on the Sabbath, in 1718. [RE.2.330]

ROBERTSON, DOUGAL, in Milntown, was admitted as a burgess of Elgin in 1760, son of Provost Robertson. [EBR]

ROBERTSON, GEORGE, jr., a merchant in Portsoy, testament, 25 May 1781, Comm. Aberdeen. [NRS]

ROBERTSON, GEORGE, a Lieutenant of the Royal Navy, died in Banff on 27 September 1799. [SM.XL.724]

ROBERTSON, ......, son of Provost Robertson, was admitted as a burgess of Elgin in 1761. [EBR]

ROBERTSON, JAMES, of Bishopmill, Provost of Elgin, from 1752 to 1755, 1758 to 1761, 1764 to 1767. [RE.2.477]

ROBERTSON, JAMES, a merchant in Jamaica, son of James Robertson of Bishopmills, a sasine, 1740. [NRS.RS29.6.449]

ROBERTSON, JAMES, in Fordyce, 1753. [NRS.E326.1.17]

ROBERTSON, JAMES, jr., a merchant in Portsoy, testament, 25 May 1781, Comm. Aberdeen. [NRS]

THE PEOPLE OF MORAY, BANFF, AND NAIRN, 1700-1799

ROBERTSON, JAMES, in Jamaica, sasines, 1784, 1788. [NRS.RS.Elgin.88/211]

ROBERTSON, JOHN, from Banff, applied for Citizenship of Bergen, Norway, in 1636. [Bergen City Archives]

ROBERTSON, JOHN, a merchant, Provost of Elgin, from 1734 to 1737. [RE.2.477]

ROBERTSON, JOHN, in Belly, Moray, 1748. [NRS.E326.1.17]

ROBERTSON, THOMAS, in Scotstoun, was appointed the Constable of Forglen, on 7 April 1741. [RB.409]

ROBERTSON, WILLIAM, chaplain to Lord Fraser, was appointed master of the Grammar School of Elgin in 1714. A Jacobite in 1715, captured and imprisoned in Stirling Castle [RE.2.411/439]

ROBERTSON, WILLIAM, from Banff, was admitted as a citizen of Rotterdam, Zealand, in 1729. [Rotterdam Archives]

ROBISON, GEORGE, in Bankanentim, was appointed the Constable of Cullen on 7 April 1741. [RB.409]

ROSE, ALEXANDER, a tailor, was admitted as a burgess of Elgin in 1707. [EBR]

ROSE, ANDREW, a weaver, was admitted as a burgess of Elgin in 1766. [EBR]

ROSE, CHARLES, born in Alves, Moray, a clergyman in Virginia from 1736 to his death in 1761. [SA.31]

ROSE, HUGH, of Kilvarock, a deed, 1706. [NRS.GD36.25]

ROSE, HUGH, a wheelwright, was admitted as a burgess of Elgin in 1760. [EBR]

ROSE, JOHN, from Forres, settled in Essex, America, before 1747, a letter to his wife in Forres. [NRS.RH1.2.861]

# THE PEOPLE OF MORAY, BANFF, AND NAIRN, 1700-1799

ROSE, ROBERT, born in Alves, Moray, on 12 February 1704, a minister in Essex County, Virginia from 1727 to 1748, and in Albemarle County, Virginia, from 1748 to his death in 1751. [SA.31]

ROSS, HUGH, of Kilravock, sasines, 11 February 1708 and 14 December 1713. [NRS.RS28.94.66; RS16.104.383]

ROSS, JOHN, an advocate in Aberdeen, was admitted as a burgess of Elgin in 1784. [EBR]

ROSS, ROBERT, a staymaker, was admitted as a burgess of Elgin in 1775. [EBR]

ROSS, WILLIAM, sometime a soldier of the 47$^{th}$ Regiment, residing in Banff, testament, 18 April 1788, Comm. Aberdeen. [NRS]

ROUST, ALEXANDER, session clerk of Elgin, was admitted as a burgess of Elgin in 1711. [EBR]; formerly professor of music in Aberdeen, was appointed master of the music school in Elgin in 1711. [RE.2.411]

ROY, ALEXANDER, was admitted as a burgess of Elgin in 1685. [EBR]

ROY, GEORGE, born 1751 in Banffshire, 'an early settler of Halifax', died in Merigomish, Halifax, Nova Scotia, in 1831. [GM.101.477]

ROY, JAMES, a wright in Elgin in 1699. [RE.2.324]]

RUDDACH, GEORGE, a vintner in Portsoy, testament, 15 November 1788, Comm. Aberdeen. [NRS]

RUDDACH, JOHN, at Montego Bay, Jamaica, was admitted as a burgess of Banff in 1800. [BBR]

RUDDIMAN, JOHN, in Bog of Montblairy, was appointed the Constable of Alva on 7 April 1741. [RB.409]

RUNCEY, GEORGE, was admitted as a burgess of Elgin in 1753. [EBR]

RUSSEL, ERROL, born 1773, son of Thomas Russel of Rathen and his wife Anna Innes, a Royal Marine Lieutenant, died in the West Indies in July 1795. [Banff gravestone]

RUSSELL, JAMES, servant to baillie Leslie, was admitted as a burgess of Elgin in 1775. [EBR]

RUSSELL, JOHN, of Rathen, a merchant in Banff, testament, 27 February 1766, Comm. Aberdeen. [NRS]

RUSSEL, RODDAM, born 1781, son of Thomas Russel of Rathen and his wife Anna Innes, a midshipman, died at Santo Domingo on 31 October 1797. [Banff gravestone]

RUSSEL, THOMAS, born 1772, son of Thomas Russel of Rathen and his wife Anna Innes, died in Martinique in July 1794. [Banff gravestone]

SANDERS, JOHN, a late merchant in Elgin bequeathed £100 for the poor in 1742. [RE.2.330]

SANDERSON, JOSEPH, minister of Alves from 1702 until 1727. [F.6.376]

SANGSTER, PATRICK, skipper in Gardenston, commander of the sloop Happy Return, testament, 19 April 1773, Comm. Aberdeen. [NRS]

SAUNDERS, Dr JAMES, a physician in Banff, testament, 20 September 1779, Comm. Aberdeen. [NRS]

SCOTT, CHARLES, in St Fergus, Banffshire, 1757. [NRS.E326.1.17]

SCOTT, JAMES, a cleric in Prince William county, Virginia, son of Reverend John Scott of Lochs in Dipple, a sasine, 1712. [NRS.RS29.Elgin.5.228]

SCOTT, JOHN, a tobacconist in Nairn, was admitted as a burgess of Elgin in 1757. [EBR]

SCOTT, JOHN, a shoemaker, was admitted as a burgess of Elgin in 1768. [EBR]

SELLAR, WILLIAM, was admitted as a burgess of Elgin in 1782. [EBR]

SETON, MARY, daughter of David Seton, a merchant bailie of Elgin, versus Ludovick Gordon, late in Elgin, who were married in Llanbryde on 21 September 1686, a Process of Divorce, 1706. [NRS.CC8.6.126]

SHAND, JAMES, a merchant and provost of Banff, testament, 21 July 1737, Comm. Aberdeen. [NRS]

SHAND, JAMES, jr., a merchant in Banff, testament, 16 July 1765, Comm. Aberdeen. [NRS]

SHAND, JOHN, in Garmouth, a sasine, 24 January 1717. [NRS.RS28.110.246]

SHANKS, JOHN, a squarewright, was admitted as a burgess of Elgin in 1757. [EBR]; in 1763. [RE.2.345]

SHANKS, JOHN, a shoemaker, was admitted as a burgess of Elgin in 1789. [EBR]

SHARP, JAMES, a wright, was admitted as a burgess of Elgin in 1784. [EBR]

SHAW, ALEXANDER, was admitted as a burgess of Elgin in 1782. [EBR]

SHAW, DAVID, born 1728 in Elgin, son of Reverend Lachlan Shaw and his wife Helen Stuart, emigrated aboard the brig <u>Lovely Jane</u> bound for New York in 1759, a merchant in New York, died there on 1 October 1767, buried in Hackensack churchyard, New York. [ANY.I.84][F.6.390]

SHAW, JAMES, servant to William King of Newmiln, was admitted as a burgess of Elgin in 1749. [EBR]

SHAW, LACHLAN, born 27 January 1729 in Elgin, son of Reverend Lachlan Shaw and his wife Helen Stuart, emigrated to Jamaica, died in London. [F.6.390]

SHEARER, ALEXANDER, a merchant, was admitted as a burgess of Elgin in 1770. [EBR]

SHEPHERD, GEORGE, visitor of the flesh-market, was admitted as a burgess of Elgin in 1781. [EBR]

SHEPHERD, WILLIAM, formerly schoolmaster at Auldearn, was appointed master of the Elgin Grammar School in 1716. [RE.2.413]

SHERAR, JOHN, born 1792 in Banffshire, died in Westminster, Ontario, on 11 February 1872. [AJ.6480]

SHERIFF, ALEXANDER, a master of Elgin Grammar School, settled in Jamaica in 1765. [Elgin Town Council minutes, 24.10.1765]

SIBBALD, JAMES, an Episcopalian minister in Keith, a Jacobite in 1715. [JNE.35]

SIM, JAMES, born 11 November 1759 in Banff, late of St Vincent, died 27 May 1825, husband of Elizabeth McKilligan, born 1761, died 1826. [Banff gravestone]

SIM, JAMES GEORGE, born 4 March 1804 in Banff, a physician on Honourable East India Company Service, died in Singapore on 10 September 1830. [Banff gravestone]

SIM, JOHN, born 1744, late of Antigua, died 29 November 1807, husband of Mary Stephen, born 1755, died 1847. [Banff gravestone]

SIMPSON, ANDREW, a merchant in Garmouth, was admitted as a burgess of Elgin in 1776. [EBR]

SIMPSON, GEORGE, was admitted as a burgess of Elgin in 1782. [EBR]

SIMPSON, GEORGE, a clerk in Kingston, Jamaica, son of George Simpson a merchant in Elgin, a deed, 1788. [NRS.RD4.244.318]

SIMPSON, JAMES, in Tobago, was admitted as a burgess of Banff in 1773. [BBR]

SIMSON, JOHN, servant to John Roy in Forres, was admitted as a burgess of Elgin in 1709. [EBR]

SIMPSON, JOHN, born 1799, son of Alexander Simpson and his wife Jean Smith, died in Canton, China, on 10 November 1822. [Banff gravestone]

SIMPSON, PETER, master of the Happy Return of Banff bound from Banff to Trontheim, Norway, in April 1807. [NRS.E504.5.1]

SIMPSON, WILLIAM, a tailor in Gerbity, Dundurcas, married Janet Winchester on 16 February 1759, emigrated with family from Rothes to Canada aboard the John and Elizabeth in 1775, were shipwrecked in the Flat River, Prince Edward Island. [TIM.18.30]

SIMPSON, WILLIAM, a weaver, was admitted as a burgess of Elgin in 1775. [EBR]

SIMPSON, WILLIAM, in Aberdeen, was admitted as a burgess of Elgin in 1783. [EBR]

SIMPSON, WILLIAM, a carpenter in the Catherine's parish, Middlesex County, Jamaica, son of George Simpson a merchant in Elgin, a deed, 1788. [NRS.RD4.244.318]

SINCLAIR, GEORGE, from Elgin, and Maria Thomson from Viljmen, Netherlands, were married in Rotterdam, Zealand, on 14 August 1712. [Rotterdam Archives]

SINCLAIR, WILLIAM, a tailor, was admitted as a burgess of Elgin in 1708. [EBR]

SKEEN, JAMES, a chapman, son of Andrew Skeen the beadle, was admitted as a burgess of Elgin in 1755. [EBR]

SKENE, ANDREW, minister at Banff, testament, 17 May 1793, Comm. Aberdeen. [NRS]

SMEILL, HENRY, a farmer, was admitted as a burgess of Elgin in 1718. [EBR]

SMITH, ALEXANDER, an Episcopalian minister in Bellie, a Jacobite in 1715. [JNE.36]

THE PEOPLE OF MORAY, BANFF, AND NAIRN, 1700-1799

SMITH, ALEXANDER, a smith, was admitted as a burgess of Elgin in 1753 [EBR]

SMITH, ALEXANDER, a shoemaker, was admitted as a burgess of Elgin in 1797. [EBR]

SMITH, EDWARD, from Fochabers, settled at Slave Lake, North America, a sasine, 1812. [NRS.RS.Elgin.827]

SMITH, GEORGE, from Portsoy, a seaman aboard the Dolphin of Philadelphia which was captured by Algerian pirates and the crew imprisoned in Algiers in July 1785. George Smith was still in captivity in July 1790. [AJ.2230]

SMITH, GEORGE, from Fochabers, settled at Slave Lake, North America, a sasine, 1812. [NRS.RS.Elgin.827]

SMITH, JAMES, a blacksmith in Cullen, testament, 18 May 1739, Comm. Aberdeen. [NRS]

SMITH, JAMES, farmer at Myreside, was admitted as a burgess of Elgin in 1752. [EBR]

SMITH, JAMES, a tailor, was admitted as a burgess of Elgin in 1756. [EBR]

SMITH, JEAN, born in Fordyce, a housekeeper in Gothenburg, Sweden, from 1759, married Peter Engstrom, died 1821 in Sweden. [N.S.7.1.147]

SMITH, JOHN, a blacksmith in the College of Elgin, and his son Alexander Smith, 'papists' in Elgin on 5 August 1735. [RE.2.383]

SMITH, JOHN, master of the Jean of Banff arrived in Leith from Banff in July 1749. [NRS.CS96/1788]

SMITH, JOHN, born in Forres, a merchant in New York from 1791 to 1818. [ANY.I.315]

SMITH, PATRICK, a blacksmith in Banff, testament, 12 June 1781, Comm. Aberdeen. [NRS]

THE PEOPLE OF MORAY, BANFF, AND NAIRN, 1700-1799

SMITH, THOMAS, a gardener in Forres, 1779. [NRS.GD248.533.5/73]

SMITH, WILLIAM, born 1745 son of Reverend John Smith in Meldrum, graduated MA from King's College, Aberdeen, in 1769, a schoolmaster in Strichen, minister of Alves from 1781 until his death on 26 January 1792. Husband of [1] Isabella Millar, parents of Alexander, John, Jean, [2] Katherine Robertson. [F.6.376]

SOUTAR, JOHN, Deacon of the Wrights of Elgin, a petition, 25 April 1699. [RE.2.324]

SPEEDY, PETER, a soldier from Forres, married Maertge Frerix in Schiedam, the Netherlands, on 14 June 1636. [Schiedam Marriage Register]

SPENS, GEORGE, master of the Friendship of Portsoy trading between Aberdeen, Bergen, Norway, Rotterdam, Zealand, and Belfast between 1742 and 1745. [NRS.E504.1.1]; trading between Inverness and Rotterdam in 1744, [NRS.E504.17.1]; master of the Concord of Portsoy trading with Rotterdam, Bergen, and Lisbon in 1748. [NRS.E504.1.2]; master of the Concord of Portsoy trading with Lisbon, Portugal, in 1749-1750. [NRS.E504.1.3]

SPENCE, JAMES, minister in Castle Martyrs, Ireland, son of Alexander Spence minister in Birnie, a sasine, 1710. [NRS.RS29.4.194]

SPENCE, MICHAEL, of Stankhouse, an attorney in the Court of Common Pleas in Dublin, Ireland, a sasine, 1708. [NRS.RS.29.4.231]

SPIDIMAN, PATRICK, a soldier from Forres, married Janniken Hutson in Schiedam, the Netherlands, on 13 June 1637. [Schiedam Marriage Register]

SQUIRE, FRANCIS, in Nairn, a bond, 21 July 1779. [NRS.RD3.238/2.106]

SQUYRE, JOHN, born 1685, educated at Edinburgh University, a missionary in Carolina from 1713 to 1718, died in Forres on 27 January 1758. [F.6.422]

STEPHEN, JAMES, in Cullen, testament, 17 October 1740, Comm. Aberdeen. [NRS]

STEEL, JOHN, a wright, was admitted as a burgess of Elgin on 21 September 1765. [EBR]

STEVEN, ALEXANDER, in Tobago, a sasine, 1795, [NRS.RS.Banff.336]

STEPHEN, DAVID, a chapman in Kineddar, was admitted as a burgess of Elgin in 1720. [EBR]

STEPHEN, JAMES, a milnwright, was admitted as a burgess of Elgin in 1760. [EBR]

STEPHEN, THOMAS, a merchant, Provost of Elgin, from 1770 to 1771. [RE.2.477]

STEPHENS, WILLIAM, agent for the York Buildings Company, a sasine, Elgin and Forres, 1731. [NRS.RS3.136.336]

STEVENSON, ELSPET, in Cullen, testament, 31 May 1722, Comm. Aberdeen. [NRS]

STEVENSON, ISOBEL, daughter of John Stevenson an apothecary in Banff, testament, 2 June 1748, Comm. Aberdeen. [NRS]

STEVENSON, JAMES, son of William Stevenson the minister at Fordyce, a sasine, 1 October 1706. [NRS.RS16.90.81]

STEVENSON, JOHN, a skipper from Portsoy, an assessor of the Scots Court in Veere, Zealand in 1738. [NRS.RH11.2]

STEVENSON, JOHN, in Fordyce, 1753. [NRS.E326.1.17]

STEVENSON, PATRICK, master of the William of Portsoy arrived in Leith from Portsoy in August 1749. [NRS.CS96/1788]; master of the Margaret of Portsoy trading with Bo'ness in 1751. [NRS.E504.1.3]

STEWART, ALEXANDER, master of the Pretty Peggy of Banff trading with Bergen, Norway, in 1752. [NRS.E504.1.4]

STEWART, ALEXANDER, of Auchluncart, Boharm, 1757. [NRS.E326.1.17]

STEWART, CHARLES, a merchant in Keith, a sederunt book, 1790-1791. [NRS.CS96.4245]

STEWART, DAVID, born 1712, a surgeon in Cromdale, emigrated via Inverness aboard the Prince of Wales bound for Georgia on 20 October 1735. [ESG.97]

STEWART, FRANCIS, son of Francis Stewart, brother of Charles the Earl of Moray, in Colonel Ligonier's Regiment of Horse, a sasine, Elgin and Forres, 1735. [NRS.RS3.148.57]

STEWART, GRISSELL, spouse of John Anderson of Mathiemilne, a sasine, Elgin and Forres, 1724. [NRS.RS3.122.118]

STEWART, JAMES, a merchant in Cullen, testament, 10 October 1746, Comm. Aberdeen. [NRS]

STEWART, JOHN, of Drummin, a sasine, Banff, 1723. [NRS.RS3.120.379]

STEWART, JOHN, master of the Happy Janet of Portsoy trading with Newcastle, England, and Cadiz, Spain, in 1749-1751, also with Kristiansand, Norway, in 1753. [NRS.E504.1.3/4]

STEWART, JOHN, a Colonel in the service of the United Provinces, brother of James Stewart, 8$^{th}$ Earl of Moray, a sasine, 1760. [NRS.RS29.7.416]

STEWART, PETER, from Banffshire, a member of the Scots Charitable Society of Boston, Massachusetts, in 1759. [NEHGS/SCS]

STEWART, ROBERT, a merchant and provost of Banff, testament, 24 February 1747, Comm. Aberdeen. [NRS]

STEWART, THOMAS, in Alva, 1748. [NRS.E326.1.17]

STEWART, WALTER, of Itlan, a sasine, Banff, 1724. [NRS.RS3.122.415]

# THE PEOPLE OF MORAY, BANFF, AND NAIRN, 1700-1799

STEWART, WILLIAM, in Bynnes, a sasine, Elgin and Forres, 1724. [NRS.RS3.122.116]

STEWART, WILLIAM, of Aswanly, formerly a merchant in Gothenburg, Sweden, later in Elgin, husband of Barbara King, a sasine, 1760. [NRS.RS29.7.389]

STRACHAN, ALEXANDER, in Finnon, was appointed Constable in Gamrie on 7 April 1741. [RB.409]

STRACHAN, Dr ALEXANDER, a physician in Banff, testament, 12 August 1763, Comm. Aberdeen. [NRS]

STRACHAN, JOHN, in Burnmouth, was appointed the Constable of Cullen on 7 April 1741. [RB.409]

STRACHAN, PATRICK, of Glenkindie, a sasine, Banff, 1724. [NRS.RS3.122.21]

STRACHAN, WILLIAM, in Buchraigie, was appointed the Constable of Boyndly on 31 May 1738. [RB.408]

STRACHAN, WILLIAM, from Banff, was admitted as a citizen of Rotterdam, Zealand, on 14 May 1754, [Rotterdam Archives]; formerly a merchant in Rotterdam, late in Banff, testament, 22 July 1777, Comm. Aberdeen. [NRS]

STRAITON, ALEXANDER, in Dordrecht, Holland, was admitted as a burgess of Banff in 1776. [BBR]

STRONACH, JOHN, a farmer, was admitted as a burgess of Elgin on 21 September 1765. [EBR]

STUART, ALEXANDER, from Banff, was admitted as a citizen of Rotterdam, Zealand, on 13 October 1733. [Rotterdam Archives]

STUART, Reverend JAMES, late of Carolina, was admitted as a burgess of Banff in 1783. [BBR]

STUART, JEAN, a 'papist in Elgin', spouse to James Gordon a merchant in Elgin, on 5 August 1735. [RE.2.383]

STUART, JOHN, a tack of Delphaber, Duthil, 1778. [NRS.GD248.533.3.56]

STUART, ROBERT, Provost of Banff, in 1724. [RB.401]

STUART, WILLIAM, a shoemaker, was admitted as a burgess of Elgin in 1768. [EBR]

STUART, WILLIAM, born 1771 in Inverugie, Moray, died in Morne Delice, Grenada, on 21 August 1845. [AJ.5099]

SUTHERLAND, ALEXANDER, of Kinminity, a sasine, Banff, 1735. [NRS.RS3.148.2]

SUTHERLAND, CATHERINE, daughter of Robert Sutherland in Elgin, versus Andrew Dunbar, son of Robert Dunbar in Peterhead her spouse, who were married in St Geill's, Elgin, in December 1667, a Process of Divorce, 1677. [NRS.CC8.6.20]

SUTHERLAND, DAVID, a glover, was admitted as a burgess of Elgin in 1703. [EBR]

SUTHERLAND, DAVID, of Kinsterie, chamberlain to Lord Duffus, a sasine, 1725. [NRS.RS3.126.124]

SUTHERLAND, JAMES, was admitted as a burgess of Elgin in 1694. [EBR]

SUTHERLAND, JAMES, son of Alexander Sutherland a seaman in Inverness, was admitted as a burgess of Elgin in 1706. [EBR]

SUTHERLAND, WILLIAM, of Mostowie, Provost of Elgin, 1705 to 1708. [RE.2.477]

SUTHERLAND, WILLIAM, a merchant in Clyth, was admitted as a burgess of Elgin in 1711. [EBR]

SUTTER, ALEXANDER, tacksman of Marcassie, 1800. [NRS.CS228.B11.46]

SYME, WILLIAM, a bailie of Banff in 1724. [RB.402]

TAES, JOHN, a merchant in Banff, testament, 10 February 1747, Comm. Aberdeen. [NRS]

TARRAS, JAMES, in Elgin, to Tangiers, Morocco, in 1678. [RPCS.X.546]

TARRAS, JAMES, a merchant in Portsoy, testaments, 1744/1748, Comm. Aberdeen. [NRS]

TARRAS, JOHN JACOB, son of Laurence Tarras, a merchant in Gothenburg, Sweden, was admitted as a burgess of Banff in 1802. [BBR]

TARRAS, ROBERT, a church elder in Elgin in 1709. [RE.2.328]

TAYLOR, BETTY, from Elgin, wife of John Moore, settled in Moresville, Delaware County, New York, in 1772. [NYGBR.25]

TAYLOR, FRANCIS, was admitted as a burgess of Elgin in 1782. [EBR]

TAYLOR, GEORGE, in Keith, 1757. [NRS.E326.1.17]

TAYLOR, ISABEL, banished from Elgin for scandalous behaviour with bailie John Donaldson, in 1706. [RE.2.327]

TAYLOR, JAMES, a merchant in Thornshill of Birnie, was admitted as a burgess of Elgin in 1773. [EBR]

TAYLOR, JAMES, a weaver, was admitted as a burgess of Elgin in 1789. [EBR]

TAYLOR, JAMES, from Fochabers, applied to settle in Canada in 1815. [NRS.RH9]

TAYLOR, JOHN, a wright, was admitted as a burgess of Elgin in 1757. [EBR]

TAYLOR, WILLIAM, in Newton of Park, was appointed the Constable of Ordequhill on 31 May 1738. [RB.408]

THOMSON, ALEXANDER, master of the Jean of Forres trading between Rotterdam, Zealand, and Inverness in 1745. [NRS.E504.17.1]

THE PEOPLE OF MORAY, BANFF, AND NAIRN, 1700-1799

THOMSON, JAMES, was admitted as a burgess of Elgin in 1719. [EBR]

THOMSON, JOHN, a weaver in Burghsea, was admitted as a burgess of Elgin in 1762. [EBR]

THOMSON, JOHN, in Forres, 1777. [NRS.CS238.T2.25]

THOMSON, JONATHAN, was admitted as a burgess of Elgin in 1719. [EBR]

THOMSON, WILLIAM, a cess-collector at Cullen, a Jacobite in 1715. [JNE.38]

THOMSON, WILLIAM, born 1786, son of John Thomson, a feuar in Dufftown, and his wife Jane Grant, died in Jamaica in 1811. [Aberlour gravestone]

THORN, DAVID, servant to baillie Leslie, was admitted as a burgess of Elgin in 1775. [EBR]

TOD, HUGH, chamberlain to the Earl of Huntly, was admitted as a burgess of Elgin in 1716. [EBR]

TOD, ROBERT, son of William Tod, [1745-1821], and his wife Helen Ogilvie, [1746-1824], surgeon of the $1^{st}$ Light Dragoons, died in Kara, Bombay, India, on 20 February 1824. [Bellie gravestone]

TOWACH, JOHN, minister in Aberlour, 1757. [NRS.E326.1.17]

TROUP, JAMES, a chapman, was admitted as a burgess of Elgin in 1760. [EBR]

TROUP, JAMES, late of Jamaica, a sasine, 15 March 1785. [NRS.RS.Elgin and Forres.120]

TULLOH, ROBERT, born 1763, son of Robert Tulloh of Bogton, Forres, a soldier in the Bengal Army, died in Calcutta, India, on 6 May 1802. [BA.4.321]

TULLOCH, ALEXANDER, a surgeon apothecary in Forres, a sasine, 7 December 1716. [NRS.RS28.110.147]

TULLOCH, ELSPETH FORSYTH, widow of Patrick Tulloch a merchant in Forres, and spouse of John Dunbar the sheriff depute of Moray, sasines, 7 December 1716. [NRS.RS28.110.147; RS28.110.150]

TULLOCH, PATRICK, a merchant in Forres, a sasine, 7 December 1716. [NRS.RS28.110.147]

TULLOCH, THOMAS, of Tannachie, a sasine, Banff, Elgin and Forres, 1722. [NRS.RS3.120.26]

TULLOCH, WILLIAM, a chapman, was admitted as a burgess of Elgin in 1760. [EBR]

TURNBULL, Mrs, from Fochabers, died in Demerara on 1 February 1801. [Glasgow Courant.1519]

TURNER, JOHN, master of the Triton of Banff trading between Aberdeen and Kristiansand, Norway in 1743 and 1744, and between Aberdeen and Belfast, Ireland, in 1745. [NRS.E504.1.1]; trading between Newcastle, England, and Inverness in 1746, [NRS.E504.17.1]; master of the Helen of Banff trading with Lisbon, Portugal, 1749-1750, and with Norway 1751-1752. [NRS.E504.1.3/4]

TWEED, ALEXANDER, son of William Tweed [1683-1760], a merchant in Banff, and his wife Jean Jaffrey, [1692-1769], a merchant in Carolina, was admitted as a burgess of Banff in 1776. [BBR][Banff gravestone]

TWEED, JAMES, master of the Jean of Banff trading with Rotterdam, Zealand, in 1750. [NRS.E504.1.3]

URQUHART, AGNES, and her daughter, charmers or witches in Elgin in 1725. [RE.2.379]

URQUHART, DANIEL, master of the Jean of Forres trading between Kirkcaldy, Fife, and Inverness in 1745. [NRS.E504.17.1]

URQUHART, Captain ROBERT, of Burdsyards, a sasine, Elgin and Forres, 1729. [NRS.RS3.134.63]

VASS, LAUCHLAN, a merchant in Forres, business records, 1765-1769. [NRS.CS96.1153-1156]

WALKER, JAMES, the Episcopal minister at Fochabers, married Miss Anderson, daughter of the late Roberts Anderson, a merchant in Fochabers, on 15 September 1798. [SM.XL.652]

WALLACE, GEORGE, a merchant in Banff, applied for citizenship of Bergen, Norway, in 1711. [Bergen City Archives]

WALLACE, JAMES, a merchant in Banff, applied for citizenship of Bergen, Norway, in 1727. [Bergen City Archives]

WALWOOD, Captain, was admitted as a burgess of Elgin in 1700. [EBR]

WARDEN, JAMES, a chapman, was admitted as a burgess of Elgin in 1798. [EBR]

WATSON, JAMES, a merchant in Cullen, trading with Bergen, Rotterdam, Bilbao, Danzig, Gothenburg, Bordeaux, Dunkirk, and Veere, 1758-1769. [NRS.CSS96.2918]

WATSON, JAMES, in Coltfield, was admitted as a burgess of Elgin in 1771. [EBR]

WATSON, JAMES, was admitted as a burgess of Elgin in 1782. [EBR]

WATSON, JOHN, servant to Robert Leslie a baillie, was admitted as a burgess of Elgin in 1760. [EBR]

WATSON, JOHN, a merchant in St Petersburg, Russia, a sasine, 1780. [NRS.RS29.8.450]

WATSON, WILLIAM, master of the Unity Jean of Banff trading with Bergen, Norway, and Dunkirk, France, in 1751. [NRS.E504.1.4]

WATSON, WILLIAM, merchant in Banff, testament, 4 March 1797, Comm. Aberdeen. [NRS]

WATT, ALEXANDER, minister of Alves from 1753 until 1774. [F.6.376]

WEBSTER, GEORGE, in the Kirkton of Forglen, was appointed the Constable of Forglen on 31 May 1738, also on 7 April 1741. [RB.408-409]

WEIR, ROBERT, a gardener in Portsoy, testament, 24 June 1782, Comm. Aberdeen. [NRS]

WHYTE, WILLIAM, treasurer and burgess of Cullen, testament, 6 October 1737, Comm. Aberdeen. [NRS]

WHITRENGAM, Dr, was admitted as a burgess of Elgin in 1731. [EBR]

WILLIAMSON, ALEXANDER, son of William Williamson, a glover, was admitted as a burgess of Elgin in 1761. [EBR]

WILLISON, THOMAS, a ship's carpenter in Banff, testament, 12 May 1767, Comm. Aberdeen. [NRS]

WILSON, ALEXANDER, son of John Wilson jr, a merchant and baillie, was admitted as a burgess of Elgin in 1755. [EBR]

WILSON, ALEXANDER, in Cullen, factor to the Earl of Findlator, testament, 6 June 1789, Comm. Aberdeen. [NRS]

WILSON, ANDREW, born 1795 in Banff, died in Calcutta, India, on 16 May 1845. [Scotch Burial Ground gravestone, Calcutta]

WILSON, DAVID, in Gardenhead of Park, was appointed the Constable of Ordiewhill on 7 April 1741. [RB.409]

WILSON, DAVID, a weaver, was admitted as a burgess of Elgin in 1787. [EBR]

WILSON, GRIZEL, accused of calling her neighbour Isabel Cock a witch, in Elgin in 1702. [RE.2.326]

WILSON, JAMES, in Newton, was appointed the Constable of Alva on 7 April 1741. [RB.409]

WILSON, JAMES, master of the Margaret of Gamry trading with Kirkcaldy, Fife, in 1750. [NRS.E504.1.3]

WILSON, JAMES, son of John Wilson jr, a merchant and baillie, was admitted as a burgess of Elgin in 1755. [EBR]

WILSON, JAMES, in Calcutta, India, a sasine, 1780. [NRS.RS29.8.494]

WILSON, JAMES, son of George Wilson and his wife Margaret Phillip in Banff, died in Port au Prince, Haiti, on 20 June 1794. [Banff gravestone]

WILSON, JOHN, a shoemaker, was admitted as a burgess of Elgin in 1766. [EBR]

WILSON, PETER, born 1794, late of Aberchirder, Banffshire, died in Duke Street, Dunedin, Otago, New Zealand, on 26 March 1876. [AJ.6699]

WILSON, WILLIAM, a vintner in Keith, 1757. [NRS.E326.1.17]

WINCHESTER, ALEXANDER, a cooper, was admitted as a burgess of Elgin in 1784. [EBR]

WINCHESTER, JOHN, a church elder in Elgin in 1701 and 1709. [RE.2.325/ 328]

WINCHESTER, JOHN, a skipper in Garmouth, testament, 1812, Comm. Moray. [NRS]

WINK, WILLIAM, a weaver, was admitted as a burgess of Elgin in 1770. [EBR]

WISEMAN, ALEXANDER, a maltman in Cullen, testament, 1 November 1726, Comm. Aberdeen. [NRS]

WISEMAN, JAMES, a bailiff of Elgin, a Jacobite in 1715. [RE.2.379]

WISEMAN, JAMES, former Lieutenant Colonel of the 91$^{st}$ Regiment of Foot, residing in Banff, testament, 25 July 1800, Comm. Aberdeen. [NRS]

WOOD, ALEXANDER, a sailor in Portsoy, testament, 18 January 1743, Comm. Aberdeen. [NRS]

WOOD, GEORGE, master of the Elspeth of Portknockie arrived in Leith from Portknockie in July 1749. [NRS.CS96/1788]

WOOD, JAMES, the younger, in Hillside, was appointed the Constable of Fordyce on 31 May 1738. [RB.408]

WOOD, JAMES, master of the Neptune of Banff trading between Inverness and Gothenburg, Sweden, in 1743. [NRS.E504.17.1]; trading with Longsund, Norway, Gothenborg, Sweden, and Aberdeen in 1742-1743. [NRS.E504.1.1]; master of the Hazard of Banff trading with Rotterdam, Zealand, in 1751-1752. [NRS.E504.1.4]

WOOD, JAMES, a writer and messenger in Banff, testament, 26 July 1743, Comm. Aberdeen. [NRS]

WOOD, JOHN, master of the Unity Jean of Banff trading with Kirkcaldy, Bergen, and Rotterdam in1752. [NRS.E504.1.4]

WOOD, PETER, in Muir of Glassa, was appointed the Constable of Fordyce on 7 April 1741. [RB.409]

WOOD, SARAH, widow of Adam Panton a merchant in Banff, testament, 9 March 1762, Comm. Aberdeen. [NRS]

WOOD, WILLIAM, master of the Helen of Portknockie arrived in Leith from Portknockie in July 1749. [NRS.CS96/1788]

WRIGHT, JAMES, possibly from Grantown-on-Spey, settled in St Thomas parish, South Carolina, probate 12 June 1790, Charleston, S.C.

YOUNG, ALEXANDER, a merchant, was admitted as a burgess of Elgin in 1776. [EBR]

YOUNG, JAMES, a skipper, was admitted as a burgess of Elgin in 1682. [EBR]

YOUNG, JAMES, a merchant, was admitted as a burgess of Elgin in 1777. [EBR]

YOUNG, WILLIAM, a merchant in Auldearn, a deed, 4 February 1731. [NRS.RH8.485]


REFERENCES

AJ = Aberdeen Journal, series

ANY = St Andrews Society of New York

BA = Officers of the Bengal Army, 1758-1834

BBR = Banff Burgess Roll

DF = Dingwall Family papers

EBR = Elgin Burgess Roll

ESG = Early Settlers of Georgia

F = Fastii Ecclesiae Scoticanae, [Edinburgh]

GM = Gentleman's Magazine, series

IT = Indian Traders of the SE Spanish Borderlands, [Fla.1986]

JNE = Jacobites of North East Scotland, [Baltimore, 1997]

MCA = Marischal College, Aberdeen

MSC = Miscellaneous of the Spalding Society

NARA = National Archives Records Administration

NRS = National Records of Scotland

NS = Northern Scotland, series

NYGBR = New York Genealogical Historical Register

## THE PEOPLE OF MORAY, BANFF, AND NAIRN, 1700-1799

RB = Records of Banffshire

RE = Records of Elgin

RPCS = Register of the Privy Council of Scotland

SA = Scotus Americanus

SAB = State Archives, Bergen

SIP = Scots in Poland

SM = Scots Magazine, series

SRS = Scottish Record Society

TIM = The Island Magazine, series

TNA = The National Archives, London

www.ingramcontent.com/pod-product-compliance
Lightning Source LLC
Chambersburg PA
CBHW071225160426
43196CB00012B/2413